50 FUN THINGS TO DO IN
BARCELONA

KIDS CITY GUIDE AND TRAVEL ACTIVITY BOOK

50 FUN THINGS TO DO IN BARCELONA:
KIDS CITY GUIDE AND TRAVEL ACTIVITY BOOK

Published by Little Travel Guides, 2017
First Edition

Copyright © Sarah Berry 2017

All rights reserved. Without limiting the rights under copyright reserved above, no part of this publication may be reproduced, stored in or introduced into a retrieval system, or transmitted, in any form or by any means (electronic, mechanical, photocopying, recording or otherwise), without the prior written permission of the publisher of this book.

ISBN 978-0-6481215-0-3

For children and teenagers

Published by Little Travel Guides
44 Smith St Brunswick West Victoria 3055 Australia
email: hi.littletravelguides@gmail.com

littletravelguides.com.au

HELLO.

Welcome to your new book.

This book is a city guide and an activity book – it holds a lot of information about different places in Barcelona and it gives you fun things to do when you visit them.

Hopefully, you'll learn some interesting stuff and have a lot of fun.

WHAT YOU'LL NEED

Always take this book and a pen or pencil with you when you head out in Barcelona. You never know when you'll see something that's in the book.

For some activities you might need more than just a pen – it is worth taking a basic pencil case of things with you, like:

- coloured pencils
- sharpener and eraser
- scissors
- glue or sticky tape

HOW TO USE THIS BOOK

Some of the activities in this book need to be done while you are visiting a particular place in Barcelona. Some can be done anywhere in the city. And some can be done in your down time – at your hotel or when you are out to dinner.

Just look at the @ symbol on each page to check where you should do each activity.

Whenever you are about to head out and about in Barcelona:

1. Find out where you are going.
2. Check this book to see which activities you can do while you are there.
3. Grab your book and a pen.
4. Go out. See stuff. Do stuff. Fill in your book along the way. And have fun.

CONTENTS
(AND ACTIVITY TICK LIST)

1 HELLO BARCELONA
A few facts and figures about Spain and Barcelona

2 THE OLD TOWN
Explore the heart of the old city and learn about its history

- 01. SPOT THIS IN THE OLD TOWN ☐
- 02. BARRI GOTIC WALKING TOUR ☐
- 03. CATHEDRAL CREATURE HUNTER ☐
- 04. CATHEDRAL WORD SEARCH ☐
- 05. CIUTADELLA LANDMARKS ☐
- 06. ARC DE TRIOMF PHOTO LOCATOR ☐
- 07. WATERFRONT ALPHA-CHALLENGE ☐

3 LA RAMBLA
A look at the sights and landmarks of this famous street

- 08. FIND LA RAMBLA LANDMARKS ☐
- 09. LA RAMBLA STEP SIZES ☐
- 10. COUNT THIS CODEBREAKER ☐
- 11. FONT PLAQUE READER ☐
- 12. LA BOQUERIA MEMORY MATCH ☐
- 13. DRAW A FRUIT STALL ☐

4 GAUDI & MODERNISM
A look at the architecture of the modernists including Gaudi

- 14. SPOT THE GAUDI CREATION ☐
- 15. PALAU GUELL'S GATES ☐
- 16. ARCHITECTURE WALKING TOUR ☐
- 17. COUNTING CASA BATLLO ☐
- 18. DESIGN A CONCERT TICKET ☐
- 19. PARK GUELL TREASURE HUNT ☐
- 20. MAKE YOUR OWN MOSAIC ☐

5 SAGRADA FAMILIA
Visit Gaudi's masterpiece – Barcelona's famous church

- 21. ORIENTATION WALK ☐
- 22. SCAVENGER HUNT ☐
- 23. DRAW STAINED GLASS WINDOWS ☐
- 24. SAGRADA FAMILIA CROSSWORD ☐

IN THIS BOOK, WHEN YOU SEE A BOX WITH ARROWS BEFORE THE HEADING LIKE THIS:

>>> SAMPLE HEADING

IT'S A MINI PUZZLE THAT YOU CAN DO ANYTIME (AND IT DOESN'T HAVE ANYTHING TO DO WITH THE PAGE OR CHAPTER IT'S IN).

6. MUSEU PICASSO

Discover the gallery dedicated to the artwork of Pablo Picasso

- 25. DRAWING WITH PERSPECTIVE
- 26. STILL LIFE COUNT UP
- 27. CLASSIFY THAT PICASSO
- 28. SPOT THE DIFFERENCE
- 29. PICASSO-STYLE PORTRAIT
- 30. PIGEON MATHEMATICS
- 31. PICASSO SHORT STORY

7. MONTJUIC HILL

Explore the parklands and sights of Montjuic Hill

- 32. BARCELONA VIEW FINDER
- 33. MAGIC FOUNTAIN PUZZLE
- 34. PARKLAND COLOUR HUNT
- 35. PARKLAND NATURE BINGO
- 36. DRAW A MIRO-STYLE PICTURE

8. ACROSS BARCELONA

Activities that can be done across the city or anywhere at all

- 37. SPOT THAT SHAPE
- 38. ENERGY BURN CHALLENGE
- 39. FONT MASTER
- 40. PUBLIC ART TREASURE HUNT
- 41. WORDS FROM BARCELONA
- 42. TAPAS TIME
- 43. FIND CAMP NOU MAZE
- 44. DRAW A BARCELONA BUILDING
- 45. FIND ONE HUNDRED
- 46. BARCELONA ALPHABET
- 47. HOTEL OLYMPICS

9. BARCELONA FOR KIDS

A list of Barcelona's kid-friendly parks, museums and more.

10. AT THE END

Test your Barcelona knowledge and look back at your trip

- 48. BEST THINGS, WORST THINGS
- 49. MAKE YOUR MAP
- 50. BARCELONA QUIZ

11. ANSWERS & CREDITS

Answers to puzzles, thanks yous and image credits

IN THIS BOOK, THIS TYPE OF BOX >> IS A TICK BOX - TICK THE PICTURE OFF WHEN YOU'VE FOUND IT, OR TICK THE THING OFF WHEN YOU'VE DONE IT.

ON THIS PAGE, TICK OFF EACH ACTIVITY WHEN YOU'VE FINISHED IT.

CHAPTER 1

HELLO BARCELONA

HOLA!

Welcome to Barcelona!

Barcelona is a beautiful city of narrow alleyways and soaring churches, of incredible art and delicious food. You'll explore beautiful buildings and sprawling parks, interesting galleries and famous landmarks.

Learn about history in the streets of the Old Town or head to the beach for a picnic in the sunshine.

Whatever you do in Barcelona, you're sure to have a great time.

Photo, left: mosaic sculpture at Park Guell. Right: the view from Palau Nacional in Montjuic.

BARCELONA FAST FACTS

- *Barcelona is a city in the country of Spain.*
- *It is Spain's second biggest city (Madrid is the biggest city.)*
- *It is home to over 1.6 million people.*
- *Barcelona is the capital city of the region of Catalonia.*
- *It is the largest city on the Mediterranean Sea.*

Some things to know about Barcelona

Food

Tapas

Tapas are small snacks that you can order at a restaurant or bar. You can order a lot of different tapas to share as a meal with everyone at your table.

Pa amb tomaquet

A simple toasted bread with tomato and garlic – delicious just on its own.

Paella and fideua

Paella is a rice dish and fideua is a noodle dish. Both are cooked in a wide flat pan with meat or seafood and vegetables.

Churros

A fried doughnut stick which can be dipped in a warm chocolate sauce. Look out for shop signs saying 'Xurreria' or 'Churreria'.

Crema catalana

A delicious sweet baked custard dessert.

Sport

Football

FC Barcelona is a famous football team that plays in the Spanish league and European competitions.

Olympic Games

Barcelona hosted the Olympic Games in 1992.

Other stuff

Siesta

A siesta is a rest time in the early afternoon, after lunch. Many shops in Spain close for siesta.

Festivals

There is nearly always an event on in Barcelona. The biggest are Festes de la Merce in February, with street parades of giant puppets, and the Eve of Sant Joan, a huge firework party in June.

THE SPANISH LANGUAGE

LEARN SOME SPANISH

Learning some Spanish words provides a great way to talk to the local people. Making an effort to say hello, thank you and good bye in Spanish will show people that you are respectful of their country. Here are some useful Spanish words to get you started.

437 MILLION SPEAKERS

It is estimated that 437 million people across the world speak Spanish as their native language.

That makes it the second most spoken native language in the world after Mandarin Chinese.

GREETINGS

Hola	Hello
Adios	Good bye
Hasta luego	See you later

YES AND NO

| Si | Yes |
| No | No |

GOOD MANNERS

Por favor	Please
Gracias	Thank you
Da nada	You're welcome
Lo siento	I'm sorry

CHATTING

Como estas?	How are you?
Estot bien	I am fine
Yo no comprendo	I do not understand
Hablas Ingles?	Do you speak English?
Me llamo Jack	My name is Jack
Tengo diez anos	I am ten years old
Yo soy de New York	I am from New York

NUMBERS

uno	one	seis	six
dos	two	siete	seven
tres	three	ocho	eight
cuatro	four	nueve	nine
cinco	five	diez	ten

BARCELONA HAS TWO OFFICIAL LANGUAGES: SPANISH AND CATALAN.

CAN YOU LEARN TO COUNT TO TEN IN SPANISH?

BARCELONA
MAPS

ALL ABOUT SPAIN

LOCATION — Spain is a country in south-western Europe. It's next to Portugal, south of France and just across the water from Africa.

LANGUAGE — Spanish. Hola!

POPULATION — 46 million people (the world's 30th biggest population – more people than Canada, less than Kenya)

CAPITAL CITY — Madrid (which is also the largest city)

CURRENCY — The Euro

AREAS IN BARCELONA

CIUTAT VELLA
The Old Town and the centre of the city, featuring narrow alleys and old buildings

EIXAMPLE
The fancy part of town, with wide avenues and grand houses from the early 1900s

MONTJUIC
The parkland area around the highest hill in the city

GRACIA
A bohemian neighbourhood which is home to Park Guell

MAP OF BARCELONA

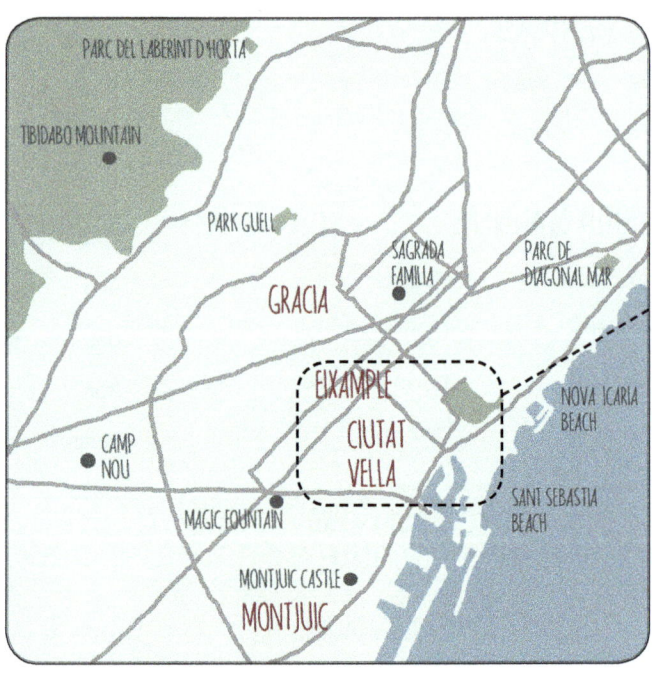

BARCELONA MAPS

MAP OF BARCELONA'S OLD TOWN

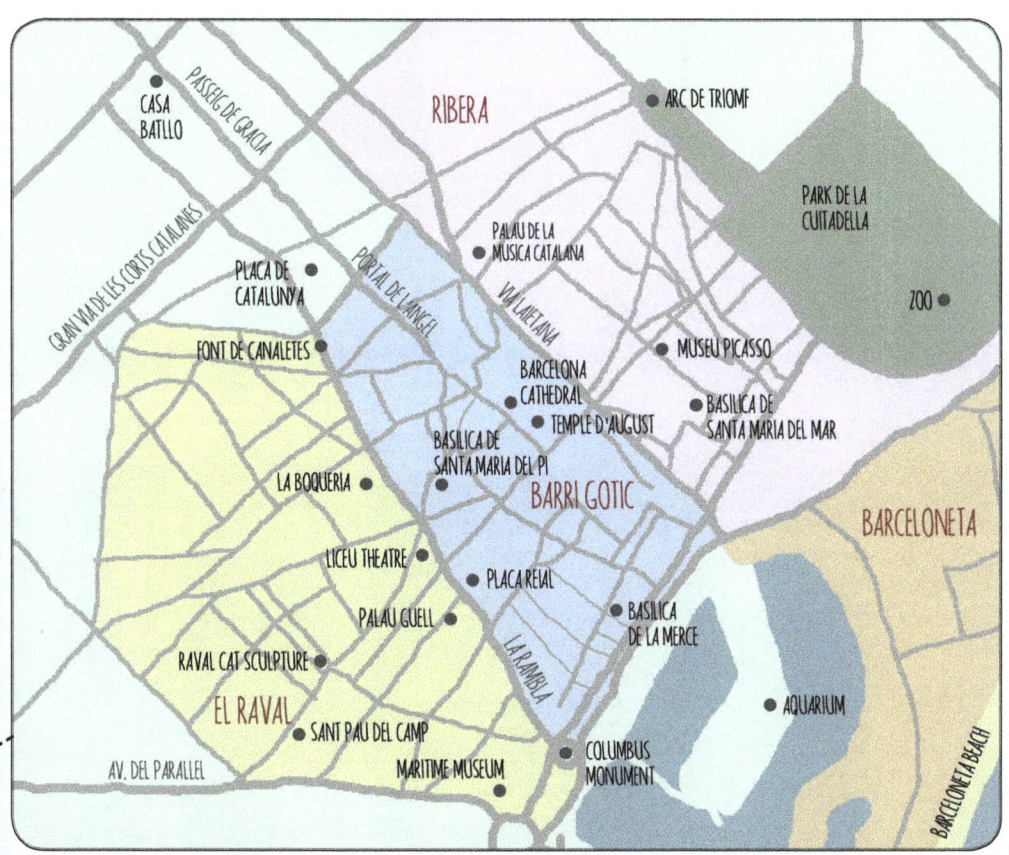

AREAS IN CIUTAT VELLA (THE OLD TOWN)

BARRI GOTIC

The centre of the Old Town with many historical sites

RIBERA (EL BORNE)

A hip area with cafes, restaurants and galleries

EL RAVAL

An vibrant and eclectic multicultural area

BARCELONETA

The port and coastal area featuring long sandy beaches

THE OLD TOWN MAP ON THIS PAGE IS A CLOSE UP OF THE BOXED AREA ON THE BARCELONA MAP ON THE FACING PAGE

CHAPTER 2
THE OLD TOWN

The Old Town is the oldest part of Barcelona, which is at the centre of the city.

It is known as 'Ciutat Vella'. 'Ciutat Vella' actually means 'Old Town'.

The Old Town is an interesting and beautiful part of the city with narrow alleys, old buildings and tons of history.

It can be hard to follow a map in the Old Town because the streets curve around and don't follow any pattern. At any moment you might wander into a big city square or a dead-end alley. That's what makes it so fun to explore.

Photo, left: Pont del Bisbe.
Right: statue of Hercules at Placa de Catalunya.

HERCULES AND THE FOUNDING OF BARCELONA

There are a few different stories about how Barcelona was founded and one of them tells a story about Hercules.

During his fourth labour, Hercules joined Jason and the Argonauts on their search for the Golden Fleece. They were travelling across the Mediterranean in nine ships when a storm blew up and one of the ships was lost. Hercules headed out to find the lost ship and discovered it wrecked on a small hill. The crew were all safe.

The crew thought the hill and its surrounds were so beautiful they decided to stay and build a city in that spot. They named their city 'ninth ship' – Barca Nona.

THE ANCIENT ROMAN CITY OF BARCINO

2000 YEARS AGO BARCELONA WAS A ROMAN TOWN CALLED BARCINO

A marble plaque from Barcino dated from 110-130 AD

The history of Barcelona stretches back over 7000 years. Information about the early settlements is scarce, but by the first century AD the Romans had built a city here called Barcino.

Barcino was laid out around a central forum and was surrounded by sturdy city walls for protection.

At the centre of the city, on a hill, was the Temple of Augustus, dedicated to Emperor Caesar Augustus. You'll visit the remains of that temple in Activity 02.

THE TEMPLE OF AUGUSTUS

Drawing of how the Temple of Augustus may have looked.

CIUTAT VELLA BUILDING TIMELINE

100 AD	Temple of Augustus built
911	The church Sant Pau del Camp was built before this time
1298	Construction of Barcelona Cathedral began
1391	Santa Maria del Pi church built
1596	The current facade on the Palau de la Generalitat built
1752	Church of Sant Felip Neri completed
1847	Gran Teatre de Liceu opened
1877	Parc de la Ciutadella established
1908	Palau de la Musica Catalana built
1913	Barcelona Cathedral's new facade built
1928	Pont del Bisbe constructed

SPOT THIS IN THE OLD TOWN

ACTIVITY 01. @ CIUTAT VELLA

KEEP YOUR EYES OPEN AROUND TOWN

How many of these twenty things can you spot while you're out and about in the Old Town?

For an extra challenge, copy the list out and give it someone else in your travelling group. Then race them to see who can spot everything on the list first.

> PORTAL DE L'ANGEL IS THE MOST WALKED ALONG STREET IN SPAIN. 3500 PEOPLE WALK IT EACH HOUR.

- ○ a person in a hat
- ○ a shop selling ice-cream
- ○ a mosaic
- ○ a dog
- ○ the word 'Barcelona'
- ○ a busker
- ○ a drinking tap
- ○ a street light
- ○ a flower stall or shop
- ○ a bicycle

- ○ a person with a suitcase
- ○ a cafe with tables outside
- ○ a bird
- ○ a person wearing yellow
- ○ an arched window
- ○ a street name sign
- ○ a statue
- ○ a shop selling bread
- ○ a blue car
- ○ a shop selling hats

BARRI GOTIC WALKING TOUR

ACTIVITY 02. @ BARRI GOTIC

 LEAD YOUR GROUP ON A TOUR OF THE OLD TOWN

Distance: about one kilometre
Time: allow an hour – there's a lot to see!
Route: starts and ends at Placa Nova

Lead your family on a walking tour of the centre of Barri Gotic. Use the map and directions to work out where to go. Stop at each point of interest and tell your group about it. The tour is designed to show you how the old town has been built and changed over hundreds of years.

*** FYI**

'Carrer' means 'street' in Catalan, so when you see the name of a street it will usually be called 'Carrer de' something.

'Placa' means 'plaza' and refers to a city square or open area.

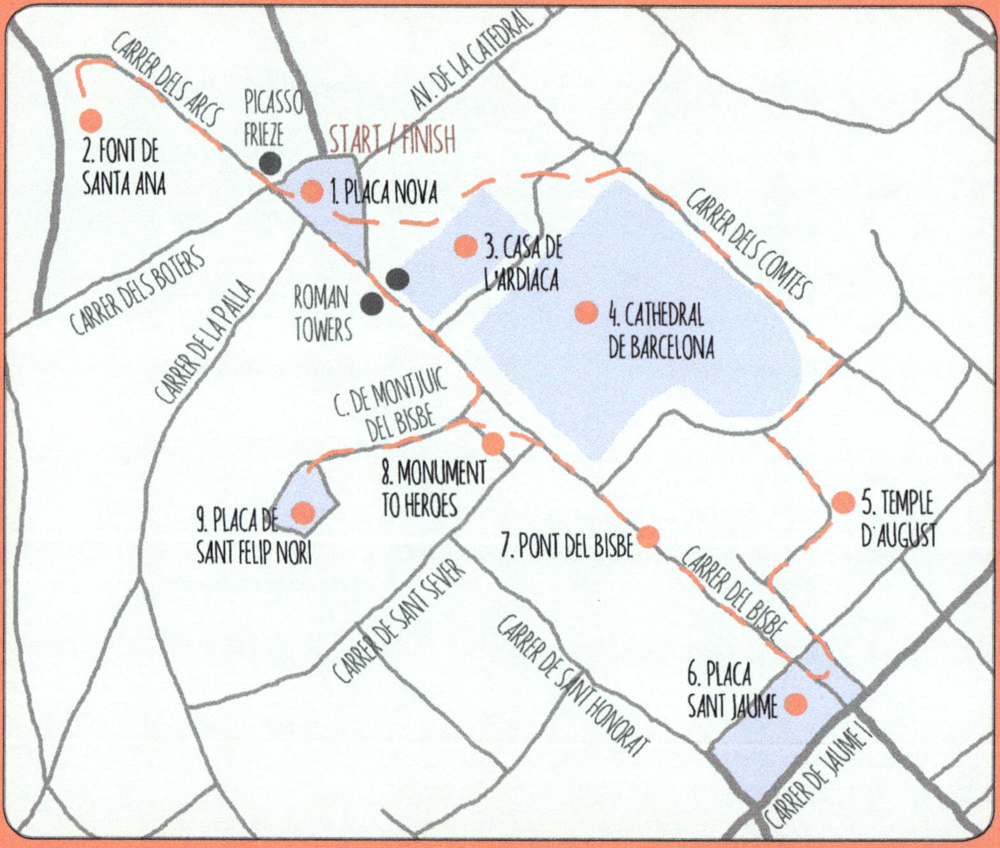

- CARRER DELS ARCS
- PICASSO FRIEZE
- AV. DE LA CATEDRAL
- START / FINISH
- 2. FONT DE SANTA ANA
- 1. PLACA NOVA
- CARRER DELS COMTES
- CARRER DELS BOTERS
- CARRER DE LA PALLA
- ROMAN TOWERS
- 3. CASA DE L'ARDIACA
- 4. CATHEDRAL DE BARCELONA
- C. DE MONTJUIC DEL BISBE
- 8. MONUMENT TO HEROES
- 9. PLACA DE SANT FELIP NORI
- 5. TEMPLE D'AUGUST
- 7. PONT DEL BISBE
- CARRER DEL BISBE
- CARRER DE SANT SEVER
- CARRER DE SANT HONORAT
- 6. PLACA SANT JAUME
- CARRER DE JAUME I

1. PLACA NOVA

TWO ROMAN TOWERS

At Placa Nova, two round towers stand on either side of the entrance to Carrer del Bisbe. The towers held the main entrance gates to the Roman city of Barcino. The towers are from the second Roman wall which was built in the fourth century AD – the second wall was built on top of the first Roman wall from first century BC.

In 1958, a section of the original Roman aqueduct was re-created – it is the archway jutting from one of the Roman towers (pictured above).

Placa Nova is also home to two pieces of public art (see Activity 40).

From Placa Nova, walk past the Picasso frieze into Carrer dels Arcs. As the street curves to your left, you'll see the Font de Santa Ana on your left.

2. FONT DE SANTA ANA

OLDEST WATER FOUNTAIN

The Font de Santa Ana was built in 1356 and it is the oldest water fountain in the city. Back in those days, people did not have running water in their homes and they came to fountains like this to fill vessels with water to take back to their homes. The fountain also had a water trough for horses to drink from. It was extended in 1819 and the coloured tiles were added in 1918.

On the tiles, can you see the year '1918' painted in Roman numerals?

COPY THE ROMAN NUMERALS FOR 1918 HERE.

Walk back down Carrer dels Arcs to Placa Nova. Casa de l'Ardiaca is the building facing Placa Nova, attached to the left-hand Roman tower.

3. CASA DE L'ARDIACA

BITS AND PIECES OF BUILDING

This building a great example of the way things change over time in a city. La Casa de l'Ardiaca was built in the 12th century on top of the old Roman walls.

Parts of the building were extended and rebuilt in the beginning of the 16th century. In 1870, the building was merged with the house next door.

In 1902, architect Lluis Domenech I Montaner redesigned the internal courtyard and designed a letterbox for the building.

The letterbox features swallows, ivy and a turtle, together symbolising the freedom of justice flying above the slow pace of the legal system.

CAN YOU FIND THE LETTERBOX?

Walk across Placa Nova to Placita de la Seu, in front of the Cathedral.

ACTIVITY 02: BARRI GOTIC WALKING TOUR – CONTINUED

 ### CATHEDRAL DE BARCELONA

A CHURCH FROM 1298

The Cathedral of Barcelona was built on the foundations of older churches that had been built on the site.

Construction on the cathedral started in 1298 – which makes it one of the oldest buildings still standing in the city. The church took over 150 years to build.

The decorative facade was added over 400 years later – work on the new facade finished in 1913. (For things to do at the cathedral, see Activity 03 and 04.)

Take the narrow road leading down the left hand side of the cathedral – Carrer del Comtes. Follow it to the back of the cathedral, then turn right down Carrer de la Pietat. Next, turn left down Carrer del Paradis. Head to the first corner, where you'll find a small sign for the Temple d'August.

 ### TEMPLE D'AUGUST

ANCIENT TEMPLE COLUMNS

At Carrer del Paradis, 10, enter through the arched doorway – hidden away in this medieval courtyard, you'll find four columns from the Roman Temple of Augustus.

This is the remains of the temple from the Roman colony of 'Barcino' which has been dated to the 1st century BC. The temple was on a hill at the centre of the settlement and looked down over the city.

These four restored columns are all that remains of the temple – the temple would have originally had six columns and measured 37 x 17 metres.

Leaving the temple, continue down the lane away from the cathedral. Follow the lane around another corner and you'll come out into Placa Sant Jaume.

PLACA SANT JAUME

OLDEST INTERSECTION

Near where you entered Placa Sant Jaume is the intersection of Carrer del Bisbe and Carrer de la Libreteria. This is one of the oldest intersections in Barcelona. The intersection was here in Roman times when these streets bordered the central forum of Barcino. The streets were called Decumanus Maximus and Cardus Maximus back then.

The Placa Sant Jaume has been at the centre of Barcelona since that time – important government buildings have been here for over 500 years. Facing this plaza, you'll see the Adjuntament de Barcelona (the town hall) and the Palau de la Generalitat de Catalunya.

Leave Placa Sant Jaume and walk down Carrer del Bisbe – back in the same direction you have come from.

 **PONT DEL BISBE**

 **MONUMENT TO HEROES**

 **PLACA DE SANT FELIP NERI**

A YOUNG-ISH BRIDGE

Do you see the ornate bridge over Carrer del Bisbe, connecting two buildings? That is Pont del Bisbe.

Architect Joan Rubio designed this little bridge to blend in with the medieval buildings. It was built in 1928 – so it is less than 100 years old. It connects the Casa dels Canonges which is 500 years old with the Palau de la Generalitat which is 400 years old.

Continue walking down Carrer del Bisbe until you come to an open area on your left (before you get back to the Roman towers). This is Placa de Garriga I Bachs.

REMEMBERING CITY HISTORY

The statue in this open plaza is called 'Monument to the Heroes of 1809'. It shows five people who were condemned to death for trying to free Barcelona from French occupation in 1809.

It was sculpted in 1929 by Josep Llimona. (Llimona also sculpted the frieze along the top of the Arc de Triomf and the Deconsol statue in Parc de la Ciutadella.)

On the plaque, can you see '1929' in Roman numerals?

COPY THE ROMAN NUMERALS FOR 1929 HERE.

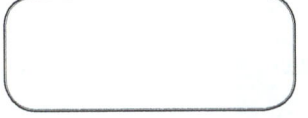

Turn left down the street at the end of Placa de Garriga I Bachs – Carrer de Montjuic del Bisbe. Walk down it until you get to the end at Placa de Sant Felip Neri.

BOMB SCARS

This quiet courtyard faces the Church of Sant Felip Neri, which was built between 1721 and 1752.

In 1938, during the Spanish Civil War, two bombs were dropped in front of the church, killing 42 people – many of them children who had been sheltering in the convent.

If you look at the walls of the church, you can see the holes in the walls that were caused by the bombings.

Head back down the street to Carrer del Bisbe and turn left. Walk between the Roman towers back to your starting point at Placa Nova. That is the end of the walking tour.

CATHEDRAL CREATURE HUNTER

ACTIVITY 03. @ BARCELONA CATHEDRAL

 CAN YOU SPOT THESE GARGOYLES ON THE OUTSIDE OF THE CATHEDRAL?

Go on a hunt for the mythical creatures that decorate the Barcelona Cathedral. Can you spot these creatures around the cathedral? Can you see any other gargoyles that look like animals or creatures?

THIRTEEN GEESE IN THE CLOISTER

The real name of the Barcelona Cathedral is 'Catedral de la Santa Creu i Santa Eulalia'. It is named for Saint Eulalia, who was a Patron Saint of Barcelona. She was thirteen years old when she died and her body was entombed in the cathedral.

A cloister is a courtyard garden in the middle of a building. This cathedral has a beautiful cloister which has a garden, a fountain, a pond – and 13 geese. There are 13 geese to remember Saint Eulalia, who was 13 years old when she died.

CAN YOU COUNT THE GEESE? ARE THERE 13?

CATHEDRAL WORD SEARCH

ACTIVITY 04. @ ANYWHERE

 FIND THESE WORDS ABOUT THE CATHEDRAL

```
L L E B J C O E O K O A E Q C
K S P I N A P S L R X S Q O R
S A W N E T A C G Y E X U X E
E I C O E H W A C E O R R S T
V N H J T E N B G H T G N V L
I T O Q R D G F S Y A U R S A
H S I A I R Z J A S P M F A R
C A R V H A F R A W A V B E G
R U B Q T L D O W L H L T E H
A A N O L E C R A B T S G N R
U E R C A T N A S Z I O X L O
N A V E S C B V C O B P W P Z
S T A I N E D R L L F R K E R
K V G E E D A C A F R A Z V R
T P Y R C U E U L A L I A T F
```

cathedral	cloister
gargoyle	geese
courtyard	naves
Barcelona	bell
archives	tower
organ	chamber
saints	choir
santa creu	facade
stained	crypt
glass	eulalia
alter	thirteen

A NEW FACADE FOR THE CATHEDRAL

The old facade of the Cathedral in the 1800s

Most of the Barcelona Cathedral was built in the 1300s. The decorative facade on the cathedral that we see today was added in 1890, over the top of the old facade.

The new facade was designed by architect Josep Oriol Mestres. Mestres also designed the Gran Teatre de Liceu on La Rambla (see Activity 08) and the water tower beside the pool in Jardin de la Torre de les Aiges in the L'Eixample area (see Chapter 9).

CIUTADELLA LANDMARKS

ACTIVITY 05. @ PARC DE LA CIUTADELLA

LOOK OUT FOR THESE LANDMARKS IN THE PARK

Parc de la Ciutadella spreads across 70 acres and holds the city zoo, museums, parliament buildings and a large fountain.

Can you find these things in the park?

The Font de la Cascada, designed by Josep Fontsere, built in 1888.

The Castell des Tres Dragons (castle of three dragons), designed by Lluis Domenech i Montaner, built in 1888.

Mammoth sculpture by Miquel Dalmau

At the Font de la Cascada – the Medallons del llangardaix, possibly designed by Gaudi when he was a young student

At the Font de la Cascada – the statue of Neptune

Deconsol sculpture by Josep Llimona in Placa de Armes

ARC DE TRIOMF PHOTO LOCATOR

ACTIVITY 06. @ ARC DE TRIOMF

IMAGINE YOU ARE THE PHOTOGRAPHER

Can you find the place that these photos were taken from? Use your hands as the photo frame and keep moving around until you have the same photo in your hand-frame.

WATERFRONT ALPHA-CHALLENGE

ACTIVITY 07. @ THE WATERFRONT AT BARCELONETA

STROLL ALONG THE BARCELONETA WATERFRONT

Take a stroll along the Barceloneta waterfront and fill in the alphabet challenge along the way.

It's a nice walk if you start at the Columbus Monument and head east along the tree-lined walkway. Turn right down Passage de Joan Borbo. At Placa del Mar, just before the cable car tower, cross over to Sant Sebastia Beach.

The walk from the Columbus Monument to Sant Sebastia Beach is two kilometres.

TIP:
KEEP A LOOKOUT FOR A FEW PIECES OF PUBLIC ART FROM ACTIVITY 40.

 TAKE THE ALPHABET CHALLENGE

On the facing page there are four letters at the top of the page. Write down one thing that you see at the waterfront for each category for each letter. (If you can't see anything that fits – or if you don't visit the waterfront – write something that you would be likely to see by the water.)

Here's an example for the letter 'L'.

Something small: little rocks

Something someone is wearing: leggings

Something in or on the water: leaves

Something you might sit on: ledge

MAKING BARCELONA'S BEACHES

Before the 1992 Olympics in Barcelona, much of the waterfront area was covered in factories. To get the city ready for the Games, the factories were moved to other areas.

The waterfront was cleaned up and sand was shipped in to convert the coast into sandy beaches. Wide footpaths, restaurants, cafes and hotels were built to complete this beachfront area.

I	C	S	B
Something small			
Something someone is wearing			
Something in or on the water			
Something you might sit on			
Something colourful			
Something you like			

CHAPTER 3
LA RAMBLA

La Rambla is a road that runs for 1.2 kilometres through the old town of Barcelona. It runs from Placa de Catalunya at the north of the old city to the Christopher Columbus Monument near the waterfront. The road forms the border between two areas of the old town – Barri Gotic and El Raval.

La Rambla is a wide street lined with trees, shops, cafes and old buildings. It is a popular street for strolling along – there are street stalls, buskers, amazing human statues and plenty of things to look at as you wander.

Photo, left: La Rambla from the Columbus Monument. Right: a 'living statue' street performer on La Rambla

A STREAM THAT TURNED INTO A STREET

In the place where La Rambla is, there used to be a stream running along the edge of the city. As the city grew, the stream became dirty and was often filled with sewerage from the city. In 1377 a construction project started to extend the old city towards El Raval. In 1440 the stream was diverted and gradually the old course of the stream became a street.

Take a look at the paving on La Rambla – it's designed in wavy ripples, to look like water – a reminder of the history of the stream before the street was here.

FIND THESE LA RAMBLA LANDMARKS

ACTIVITY 08. @ LA RAMBLA

 CAN YOU SPOT THESE LANDMARKS AS YOU WALK DOWN LA RAMBLA?

1. PLACA DE CATALUNYA

La Rambla starts at the city square called Placa de Catalunya. It is considered to be the centre of the city, where the Old Town meets the area of Eixample. The square is well known for its fountains, statues and pigeons.
(See Activity 09 and 10.)

2. FONT DE LA CANALETES

This drinking fountain is a popular meeting point and it's the place that supporters of the Barcelona Futbul Club celebrate their victories.
(See Activity 09 and 11.)

3. FONT DE LA PORTAFERRISSA

When you get to Carrer de la Portaferrissa, turn left and walk a few metres. Just near the corner you'll see the Font de la Portaferrissa – a fountain that supplied water to local houses. The ceramic tile picture of the old city walls was added in 1959.
(See Activity 11.)

TIP: YOU CAN DO ALL THE ACTIVITIES IN THIS CHAPTER AS YOU WALK DOWN LA RAMBLA.

PALAU DE LA VIRREINA

This richly decorated palace was the largest and finest house in Barcelona when it was built in the 1770s. The city council bought the building in 1944 and today it houses the city's Culture Institute. Step inside the building and you might find four of the giant puppets used for festivals on display here. (See Activity 10.)

 ## LA BOQUERIA MARKET

Barcelona's central market is called the Mercat de Sant Josep de la Boqueria (or just 'La Boqueria' for short). A Barcelona market has been around since 1217, but the market has officially been on this site since 1840. (See Activity 12 and 13.)

 ## PLA DE L'OS MOSAIC BY JOAN MIRO

Joan Miro was a famous Spanish artist who grew up in the Barri Gotic area. Miro's artwork is exhibited in galleries all over the world and there is a museum dedicated to Miro in Barcelona. You'll learn more about Miro in Activity 36. (In this chapter, see Activity 09).

 ## GRAN TEATRE DEL LICEU

The Gran Teatre del Liceu is an opera house. It was built in the 1840s – the facade and the grand hall inside are from the original building, but two fires in 1861 and 1994 destroyed most of the rest of the opera house, which has been rebuilt. (See Activity 10.)

 ## PLACA REIAL

Placa Reial (Royal Plaza) is off to the side of La Rambla. Head down Carrer de Colom and into the open square. Gaudi designed the ornate lampposts in Placa Reial. (See Activity 09 and 10.)

> **TIP:**
> Almost opposite Carrer de Colom and Placa Reial is Carrer Nou de la Rambla. Head about 50 metres down and you'll find Palau Guell, a building featured in Activity 19.

 ## COLUMBUS MONUMENT

This enormous monument is 60 metres tall. Christopher Columbus stands on the top pointing out to sea. The monument commemorates Columbus's first voyage to the Americas – he reported back to the king and queen in Barcelona after the voyage. (See Activity 09 and 10.)

LA RAMBLA STEP SIZES

ACTIVITY 09. @ LA RAMBLA

 COUNT HOW MANY STEPS IT TAKES TO WALK AROUND THESE THINGS

PLACA DE CATALUNYA

In the main area in the centre of the Placa, there is a large circle made up of six black wedges with a white border. Walk right around the border one of the black wedges. How many steps did you take?

FONT DE LA CANALETES

Walk around the font. How many steps did you take?

PLA DE L'OS MOSAIC

Walk right around the outside on the mosaic. How many steps did you take?

PLACA REIAL

Walk right around the outside of the fountain in Placa Reial. How many steps did you take?

COLUMBUS MONUMENT

Walk right around the base of the monument. How many steps did you take?

DRAW A LINE TO CONNECT EACH LANDMARK TO ITS SIZE

PLACA CATALUNYA	BIGGEST
FONT DE LA CANALETES	SECOND BIGGEST
PLA DE L'OS MOSAIC	MIDDLE SIZED
PLACA REIAL FOUNTAIN	SECOND SMALLEST
COLUMBUS MONUMENT	SMALLEST

COUNT THIS CODEBREAKER

ACTIVITY 10. @ LA RAMBLA

 COUNT THE DETAILS THEN BREAK THE CODE

PLACA DE CATALUNYA

Can you find the Frederic Mares statue of a woman on a horse holding a boat up in the air?

How many arms plus legs plus noses are there all together in this sculpture? = U

PALAU DE LA VIRREINA

How many round windows are in the top floor of the Palau facing La Rambla? = O

How many large urns are lined up along the front of the roof? = V

GRAN TEATRE DEL LICEU

How many large arched windows are there on the second floor? = N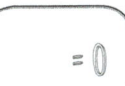

In the large arched windows, count up all the circles decorating the top of the windows. How many circles are there altogether? = L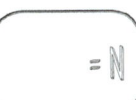

PLACA REIAL

On one of Gaudi's lampposts (with dark red features and a winged helmet on top) how many lanterns are there? = D

On one of Gaudi's lampposts, how many serpents with open mouths are wrapped around the post near the top? = E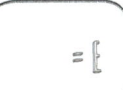

COLUMBUS MONUMENT

How many lions guard the base of the monument? = R

How many statues of Columbus stand on the very top of the column? = W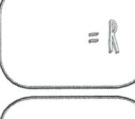

USE YOUR ANSWERS TO SOLVE THIS QUOTE PUZZLE

Spanish poet Federico Garcia Lorca once said that La Rambla was:

"the only street in the world which I wish... ____ ____ ___ "

---

1   5   15   24   6   3   2   12   2   8   2   3   6

FONT PLAQUE READER

ACTIVITY 11. @ LA RAMBLA

 ### READ THE PLAQUE AT FONT DE LA PORTAFERRISSA

Under the picture of the city walls, find the plaque that starts with the words:

"LA PORTA FERRICA" ERA UNA DE LAS PUERTAS

We will call that line the heading and there are four lines of writing under that heading.

1. In the third line, find the seventh word. Write down the second letter.

2. In the second line, find the eighth word. Write down the third letter.

3. In the first line, find the fifth word. Write down the second letter.

4. In the fourth line, find the first word. Write down the fourth letter.

5. In the first line, find the ninth word. Write down the second letter.

6. In the fourth line, find the fourth word. Write down the second letter.

7. In the heading, find the third word. Write down the first letter.

8. In the second line, find the seventh word. Write down the second letter.

WHAT DID YOU SPELL?

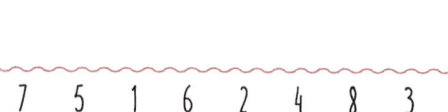

7   5   1   6   2   4   8   3

 ### READ THE PLAQUE AT FONT DE CANALETES

Find the plaque on the ground near the Font de Canaletes – it tells a popular legend about the fountain. The plaque can be translated as:

"If you drink water from the Font de Canaletes you will always be in love with Barcelona. And however far away you go. You will always return."

Looking at the Spanish words on the plaque, can you work out:

Which Spanish word means water?

Which word means love?

And do you think you'll come back to Barcelona one day?

FOUNTAIN WATCH

Font de Canaletes is famous because of the legend, but there are other fountains of exactly the same design as this around Barcelona. Keep your eyes open and try to spot them.

LA BOQUERIA FOOD MEMORY MATCH

ACTIVITY 12, PART 1. @ ANYWHERE

 ### LEARN THE SPANISH NAMES FOR FOODS

These types of foods are all sold at La Boqueria. Study the list and try to memorise the Spanish names. When you are ready, turn over the page and test your memory.

LA RAMBLA IS NOT A ROAD

La Rambla is not actually one road. It is five smaller roads that run end to end and are collectively known as La Rambla or Las Ramblas. The roads are:

- Rambla de Canaletes
- Rambla dels Estudis
- Rambla de Sant Josep
- Rambla dels Caputxins
- Rambla de Santa Monica

 banana
platano

 apple
manzana

 crab
cangrejo

 mushroom
seta

 cheese
queso

 cake
pastel

 fish
pescado

 strawberry
fresa

 lemon
limon

 egg
huevo

 chicken
pollo

 potato
patata

 bread
pan

 pineapple
pina

 carrot
zanahoria

LA BOQUERIA FOOD MEMORY MATCH

ACTIVITY 12, PART 2. @ ANYWHERE

 ### PUT YOUR MEMORY TO THE TEST

Look at this page only after you've memorised the Spanish names for the foods on the previous page.

Once you've studied them, turn to this page and try to remember the food names. Draw a line to connect each food with its name.

>>> NUMBER SEQUENCE

Can you fill in the next three numbers in these number sequences?

7, 5, 8, 4, 9, 3, ? _____

99, 92, 86, 81, 77, ? _____

2, 5, 11, 23, 47, ? _____

DRAW A FRUIT STALL

ACTIVITY 13. @ LA BOQUERIA (OR ANYWHERE)

LOOK CAREFULLY AT THE FRUIT STALLS

When you go to La Boqueria, take a close look at some of the fruit and vegetable stalls. What kind of fruits and vegetables are sold together? What are they stored in? How are they displayed? What kind of signs are used?

When you get a chance to sit down with some coloured pencils, draw one of the fruit and vegetable stalls from memory.

CHAPTER 4
GAUDI & MODERNISM

Antoni Gaudi was a Spanish artist and architect who lived in Barcelona. He is famous for his wildly creative buildings which don't follow the usual rules of symmetry and balance. They are colourful and individual – more like detailed works of art than buildings. Many of Gaudi's famous buildings are in Barcelona.

Around the 1900s, Gaudi was a part of the art movement called 'modernism'. The movement uses curves rather than straight lines and takes inspiration from nature – you will see trees, leaves and flowers in many modernist designs.

The modernist architects worked with many different craftspeople to embellish their buildings with sculpture, ceramics, stained glass, wrought iron and carpentry. Many of the modernist houses also had custom-designed furniture.

The work of Gaudi and the modernist designers is one of Barcelona's biggest tourist attractions.

BARCELONA'S WORLD HERITAGE SITES

World Heritage Sites are places that have been chosen as important landmarks for the world.

Barcelona has nine World Heritage Sites and all of them are modernist buildings. Seven of them were created by Gaudi, including Casa Batllo and the Sagrada Familia. The other two were designed by Lluis Domenech i Montaner: the Palau de la Musica Catalana and the Hospital de Sant Pau.

Photo, left: Gaudi's Casa Batllo.
Right: Ceramics at Montaner's Hospital de Sant Pau.

SPOT THE GAUDI CREATION

ACTIVITY 14. @ ACROSS BARCELONA

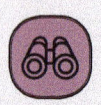

SPOT THESE WORKS BY GAUDI

When you see a Gaudi creation:

1. Draw a smiley / frowny face to show how much you like it
2. Finish the sentence about it

LAMP POSTS IN PLACA REIAL

The lamp posts for Placa Reial were one of Gaudi's earliest commissions.

These lanterns have decorations that look like...

CASA VICENS

The first house that Gaudi designed in Barcelona.

I like the way...

PALAU GUELL

A house near La Rambla with arched iron gates.

The best thing about this building is...

CASA BATLLO

A curvy house with a 'dragon's back' roof on Passeig de Gracia.

Something that makes this building unusual is...

CASA MILA (LA PEDRERA)

A curvy apartment block on Passeig de Gracia.

This building is different from other apartment buildings because...

PARK GUELL

A large park featuring lots of colourful mosaic work.

The thing I liked most in the park was...

SAGRADA FAMILIA

A large church which is considered to be Gaudi's biggest masterpiece.

This building has a lot of...

PALAU GUELL'S GATES

ACTIVITY 15. @ PALAU GUELL

ABOUT PALAU GUELL

Head down Carrer Nou de la Rambla to Palau Guell – a house that Gaudi designed for wealthy businessman, Eusebi Guell.

Guests would enter the arched gateways in their horse-drawn carriages. The horses would be taken to the stables while the guests would head upstairs to the entertaining room.

The arched iron gates have a swirling design that looks a bit like seaweed or swirling water.

DESIGN SWIRLING IRONWORK FOR YOUR OWN PALAU GATES

Imagine you have your own palau. Design the swirling ironwork to decorate your palau gate. Include your initials in your gate design – like the 'EG' in Eusebi Guell's gates.

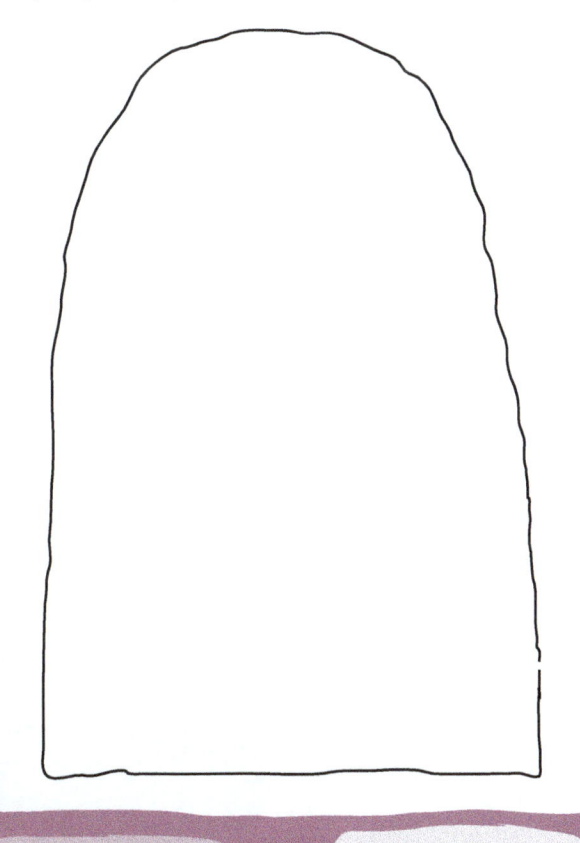

CAN YOU SEE THE SNAKE WITH HIS TONGUE STICKING OUT?

CAN YOU SEE THE LETTERS E AND G (FOR EUSEBI GUELL) SCULPTED IN THE GATES?

ARCHITECTURE WALKING TOUR

ACTIVITY 16. @ PASSEIG DI GRACIA

WALK ALONG THE MOST EXPENSIVE STREET IN SPAIN

Like La Rambla, Passeig de Gracia is a street in Barcelona that heads out from Placa de Catalunya. But Passeig de Gracia is a very different street from La Rambla – it runs through the wealthy 19th century area of Eixample and it's probably the most expensive street in Spain.

The street is famous for its architecture. It contains some of the city's most ornate buildings – houses designed by architects of the modernism movement.

Modernist architects worked with many craftspeople to create the sculptures, stained glass and ornamentation on their buildings.

TAKE THE ARCHITECTURE WALKING TOUR

Distance: 1.4 kilometres (or 2.4 kilometres if you walk on to Casa Vicens – see below)

Time: allow at least one hour

Route: Along Passeig de Gracia, from Placa de Catalunya to Carrer de Seneca

EXTRA KILOMETRE FOR AN EXTRA GAUDI HOUSE

There are two buildings on Passeig de Gracia designed by Gaudi – and you can extend your walk to include a third Gaudi house if you like.

At the end of Passeig de Gracia, continue walking for an extra kilometre to Casa Vicens, Gaudi's first house design in Barcelona.

THE BLOCK OF DISCORD

There is one block on Passeig de Gracia that holds four of the most notable houses. It is known as Illa de la Discòrdia, or the 'Block of Discord', because people felt that the four houses clashed with each other and the other houses on the street.

An old Barcelona postcard showing the Block of Discord

START THE WALK

From Placa de Catalunya, walk three blocks down Passeig de Gracia. Cross Carrer del Consell de Sent onto the 'block of discord' with its four clashing houses. The building on the corner on your left is Casa Lleo Morera.

DRAW A DETAIL

At each building on the tour, stop and draw one decoration. You could choose a swirling carved decoration or a door handle or the shape of a window – anything you like.

DRAW A DETAIL FROM EACH BUILDING IN THESE BOXES >>>

CASA LLEO MORERA

Passeig de Gracia, 35
(Corner of Passeig de Gracia and Carrer del Consell de Sant)

Designed by: Lluis Domenech I Montaner

Completed: 1906

This house is considered one of the best examples of the modernism movement. It won the Barcelona Arts Building Annual Award in 1906. This was the house of the Morera family — Morera means 'mulberry tree' and several mulberry trees can be found in the design. Can you spot any mulberry trees?

CASA MULLERAS

Passeig de Gracia, 37

Designed by: Enric Sagnier

Completed: 1906

A sturdier, squarer and less ornate house than Casa Lleo Morera, this building is in the neoclassical style. It contrasts to the curves and ornamentation of the modernist style buildings. (The architect, Enric Sagnier, also designed the church on top of Mt Tibidabo.)

ACTIVITY 16: ARCHITECTURE WALKING TOUR - CONTINUED

CASA AMATLLER

Passeig de Gracia, 41

Designed by: Josep Puig I Cadafalch

Completed: 1900

This unusual building was refurbished for Barcelona chocolate maker Antoni Amatller. The architect combined traditional craftsmanship with modern design for this angular, decorative building.

CASA BATLLO

Passeig de Gracia, 43

Designed by: Antoni Gaudi

Completed: 1906

This curving house is sometimes called the 'House of Bones'. The roof is thought to represent a dragons back and some people say that the tower is the sword of St George, plunged into the dragon's back.
(See Activity 17.)

Walk three blocks and cross Carrer de Provenca. The house on the right corner is Casa Mila.

CASA MILA (LA PEDRERA)

Passeig de Gracia, 92

Designed by: Antoni Gaudi

Completed: 1912

This building was the last private residence designed by Gaudi. The main floor was a large apartment for the Mila family and the rest of the building was apartments that were rented out. Just about everything in this building design is curved.

DON'T FORGET TO DRAW A DETAIL IN EACH BOX

👟 *Walk on two blocks to Avinguda Diagonal. You'll see Palau Robert on the left corner, a large home that is now an exhibition centre. Cross Avinguda Diagonal and continue to El Palauet on the left.*

CASA BONAVENTURA FERRER (EL PALAUET)

Passeig de Gracia, 113

Designed by: Pere Falques I Urpi

Completed: 1906

This building was known as 'El Palauet', which means 'cute little palace', because of its beauty and small size. It was a house but it has been converted into a luxury hotel called 'El Palauet'.

👟 *Walk to the end of Passeig de Gracia. On your right is Casa Fuster.*

CASA FUSTER

Passeig de Gracia, 132

Designed by: Lluis Domenech I Montaner.

Completed: 1911

This corner building has three elaborate facades in white marble and a round corner tower. When it was built, it was thought to be the most expensive building in Barcelona because of the materials used.

EXTRA KILOMETRE FOR EXTRA GAUDI HOUSE

👟 *Continue walking down Carrer Gran de Gracia for almost a kilometre to Carrer de les Carolines. Turn left and walk one block to Carrer d'Aulestia I Pijoan on the left. Casa Vicens in on the right.*

CASA VICENS

Carrer de les Carolines, 24

Designed by: Antoni Gaudi

Completed: 1885

This was the first house designed by Gaudi and it was his first chance to let his creativity loose on a whole building. It was built for Manel Vicens i Montaner, a wealthy businessman.

COUNTING CASA BATLLO

ACTIVITY 17. @ CASA BATLLO

ABOUT CASA BATLLO

Casa Batllo is a house designed by Gaudi for the Batllo family. ('Casa' means house in Spanish, so it was known as 'Casa Batllo' – 'Batllo house').

The wealthy Batllo family wanted a unique house and they did not place any limits on Gaudi – they wanted him to design something distinctive.

Look at the windows and balconies. Unlike most buildings, there are a lot of different shapes, sizes and styles of window and balcony.

COUNT THE FEATURES AND BREAK THE CODE

Look at the clues below and find the answers by looking closely at Casa Batllo.

Write your number answers in each box, then use the corresponding letters to fill in the codebreaker at the bottom of the page and solve the mystery word.

How many arched doors and windows can you count on the ground floor? = H

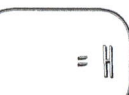

How many plain rectangle windows like this? = R

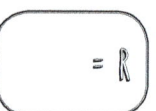

How many oval shaped holes can you count in the balcony on the top left of the building? = T

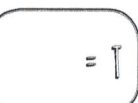

How many little round balconies like this? = I

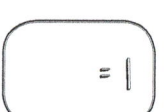

How many balconies with vertical posts like this? = C

How many balconies with two oval shapes cut out of them? = A

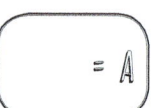

On the second floor (with no balconies) how many bone-like columns like this, in front of windows, can you count? = E

WHAT WAS GAUDI'S JOB?

7　2　4　5　1　3　6　4　3

THE CRAFTSPEOPLE WHO WORKED WITH THE MODERNISTS

GAUDI'S WORK ISN'T ALL BY GAUDI

When people see Gaudi's work, they sometimes assume that he was responsible for all of the creative design.

But Gaudi, like all the architects in the Catalan modernist movement, worked closely with a large number of craftspeople. These were people who created wrought iron, stained glass, sculpture and carpentry.

Here are three of the people who worked with the modernist architects to create their elaborate buildings.

ANTONI RIGALT I BLANCH

Antoni Rigalt i Blanch was a Catalan artist and glassmaker. He worked on many modernist houses including Casa Lleo Morera (one window pictured below) but his most famous work is the stained glass ceiling at Palau de la Musica Catalana.

JAUME PUJOL I BAUCIS

Jaume Pujol I Baucis took control of a ceramic factory in 1876 which soon became the leading supplier of ceramic tiles to the modernist architects.

The factory made pieces based on the designs supplied to them. Their tiles can be seen at Casa Amatller and Casa Lleo Morera as well as in the mosaics at Park Guell.

JOSEP MARIA JUJOL

Josep Maria Jujol was a Catalan architect. He worked with Gaudi on projects including Casa Batllo, Casa Mila and Park Guell.

At Casa Mila he was responsible for decorations in the main apartment and for finishing the decorative chimneys.

At Park Guell, Jujol decorated the mosaic benches and roof details in the trencardis mosaic technique.

THE PALAU DE LA MUSICA CATALANA

CATALAN MUSIC HALL

The Palau de la Musica Catalana is a concert hall. It was completed in 1908 for the Orfeo Catala – a Catalan music society. Today, the Palau is used for musical performances – from traditional Catalan music to jazz and classical symphonies.

THE BUILDING

The Palau de la Musica Catalana was designed by architect Lluis Domenech i Montaner. The building won a Barcelona City Council award for best building in 1909.

This building is in the modernist style. You can see the curves and rich decoration with floral motifs.

The architect gave many local craftspeople creative freedom to design decorative elements for the building in their own style – such as sculpture, mosaic and stained glass.

CAN YOU SPOT THE WORDS 'ORFEO CATALA' ON THE BUILDING?

ARCHITECT: LLUIS DOMENECH I MONTANER

Montaner was an important architect in the Catalan modernist style. As well as the Palau de la Musica Catalana, Montaner designed some other buildings that you might see in Barcelona.

- *Hospital de Sant Paul (see Chapter 10)*
- *Casa Lleo Morera and Casa Fuster (see Activity 16)*
- *Courtyard and letterbox at Casa de l'Ardiaca (see Activity 02)*
- *Castell dels Tres Dragons in Parc de la Ciutadella (see Activity 05)*

DESIGN A CONCERT TICKET

ACTIVITY 18. @ PALAU DE LA MUSICA CATALANA

FIND THESE MOSAIC TICKET WINDOWS

These windows, designed by Lluis Bru, were used to sell tickets when this was the main entry to the building.

The floral and leaf mosaic designs use simple shapes and bright colours to create a happy, lively feeling – the ticket windows feel like a good place to be.

DESIGN A CONCERT TICKET

Can you design a ticket that could be passed out of this window? It can be any shape and any design. It should feel like a happy, lively ticket – to match the window.

PARK GUELL TREASURE HUNT

ACTIVITY 19. @ PARK GUELL

THE TREASURE HUNT

Go for a walk around Park Guell. You're on the lookout for six 'treasures' – six pieces of Gaudi's artwork.

The pictures to the right are your clues – they show just a small part of each treasure.

When you find the treasures, draw each one in the correct circle on the map to show which treasure belongs in which location in the park.

After you have found the treasures make sure you explore the park thoroughly – there's a lot to see!

THE SIX TREASURES

THE STORY OF PARK GUELL: A HOUSING PROJECT THAT DIDN'T WORK

Eusebi Guell was a wealthy Barcelona businessman. He had the idea of creating a new area of luxury houses. It would be near the city but away from the factories – a place with fresh air and beautiful views.

He bought the Park Guell site in 1900 and moved into a house that was already there. Guell employed his friend Antoni Gaudi to design the site.

Gaudi designed the layout of the housing area and parkland. The terrace was to be an open area for socialising and the covered area under the terrace was for a thriving marketplace.

But only two of the new luxury houses were ever built (neither of them designed by Gaudi). No-one wanted to buy the houses and the project was abandoned.

Gaudi himself bought one of the houses and lived there for twenty years – that building is now the Gaudi House Museum.

The Guell family donated the park to the city in 1923 and it now a Municipal Garden, open to the public.

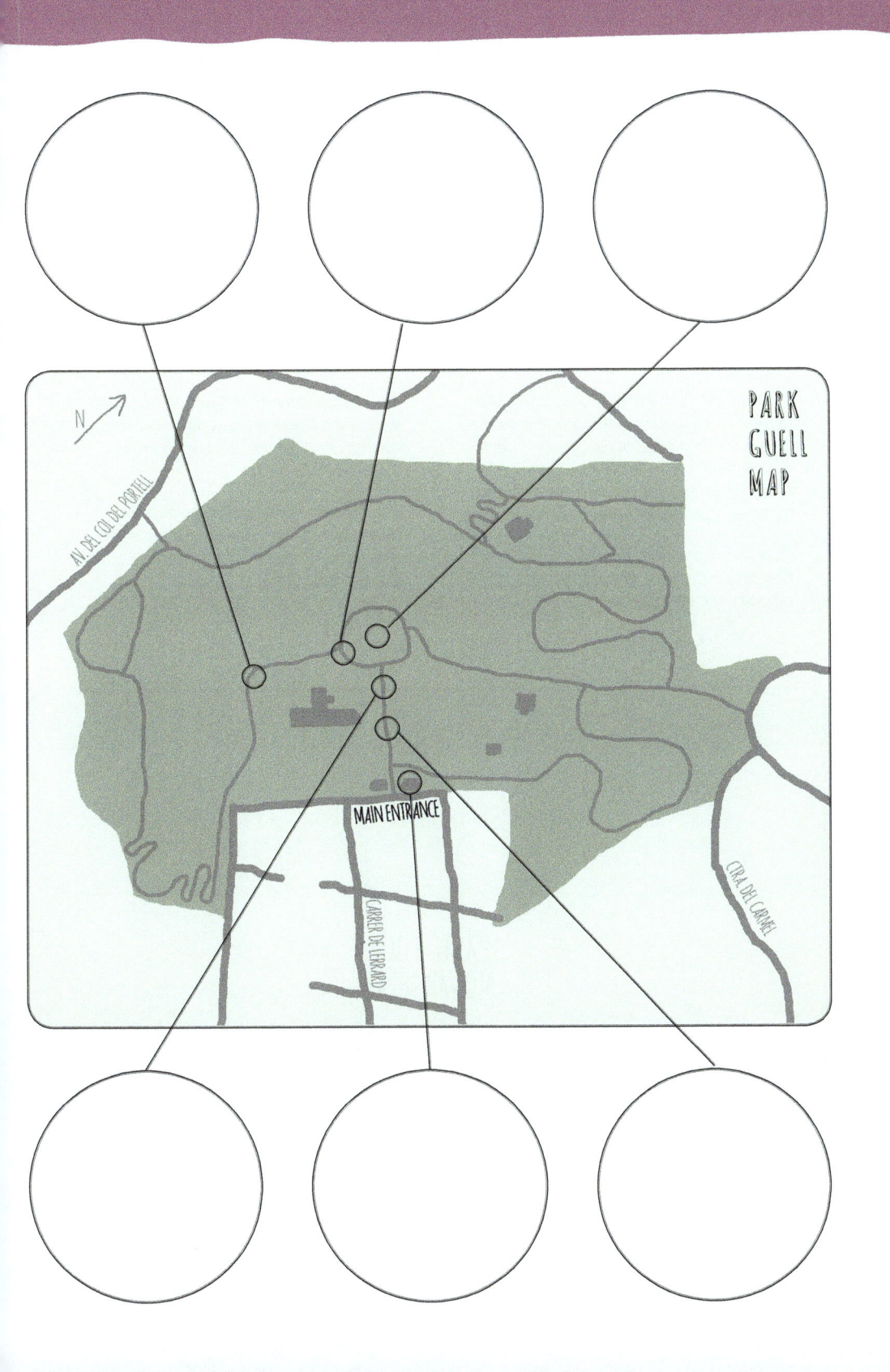

PARK
GUELL
MAP

MAKE YOUR OWN MOSAIC

ACTIVITY 20. @ PARK GUELL - AND ANYWHERE AFTERWARDS

LOOK CLOSELY AT PARK GUELL'S BENCH MOSAICS

Take a seat at one of the mosaic benches at Park Guell. Look closely at the mosaics. Can you see pieces of tile broken from the same piece, with the same design? And look at the way colours are grouped together – green with green, pink with pink.

Now step back from the bench. Look at how larger patterns are made with small pieces working together.

The mosaic technique used here is called trencardis. Trencardis is using broken pieces of pottery or ceramic to create a decorative mosaic.

The mosaic work in these benches (and most of Park Guell's mosaic work) was done by architect and artist Josep Maria Jujol.

PASTE YOUR
MOSAIC HERE

MAKE YOUR OWN MOSAIC

Draw the four pictures described in the four boxes below (or use another piece of paper if you don't want to cut your book). Cut each picture up into about six to eight pieces.

Arrange the shapes in the mosaic box on the facing page. Try to put some pieces that belong together next to each other together, in the way that you saw at Park Guell.

Glue your pieces down to create your own trencardis-style mosaic masterpiece!

CAN YOU SEE THIS PART OF MOSAIC?

This picture is a part of the mosaic from Park Guell's bench seats. Can you find where this exact section of mosaic is? (There is a clue in the answers – but only look if you really need it.)

1. A TREE - BLUES AND GREENS

2. SOME FLOWERS - PINKS AND PURPLES

3. A SUNSET - YELLOWS AND ORANGES

4. BUTTERFLIES AND BUGS - REDS AND BLACK

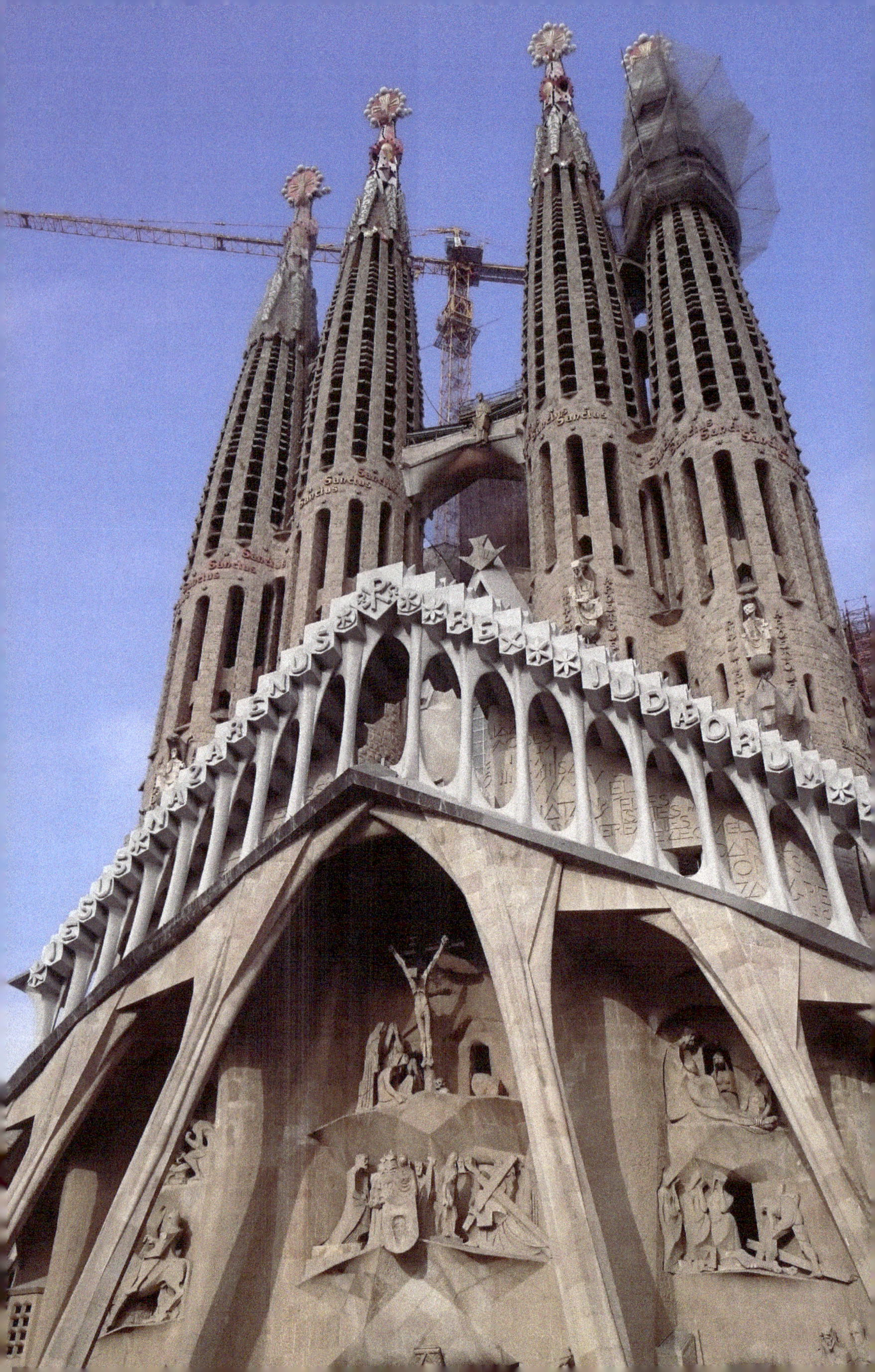
IESUS NAZARENUS REX IUDAEORUM
Sanctus Sanctus

CHAPTER 5

SAGRADA FAMILIA

The Sagrada Familia is a church in Barcelona. It is one of Spain's most-visited tourist attractions, with more than two million visitors each year.

The Sagrada Familia was designed by Spanish architect Antoni Gaudi. He had a vision for a large, elaborate, soaring church with 18 towers stretching up towards the sky. Between 1883 and 1923, Gaudi completed detailed designs for the church and all of its elements.

Construction on the church started in 1882 and it is still being built today, over 130 years later. You might see scaffolding, building materials and cranes on site. The building is expected to be finished in 2026.

The Sagrada Familia is being built according to Gaudi's vision and design, but many architects, modellers, artists, sculptors, craftspeople and builders have worked to make this beautiful building a reality.

Photo, left: the Passion Facade.
Right: A worker hanging around.

YOU ARE HELPING TO BUILD THE SAGRADA FAMILIA

The construction of the Sagrada Familia has been entirely funded by donations – the entrance fee you pay to visit the church will contribute too.

So, by visiting the Sagrada Familia YOU are helping to build it.

ORIENTATION WALK

ACTIVITY 21. @ SAGRADA FAMILIA

LEAD YOUR GROUP ON AN ORIENTATION WALK OF THE CHURCH

Take your family on a short orientation walk* around the church. You can be the tour guide and read each fact out loud to your group. Check the map of the church to see you where to stop to read each fact.

MAP OF THE SAGRADA FAMILIA ORIENTATION WALK

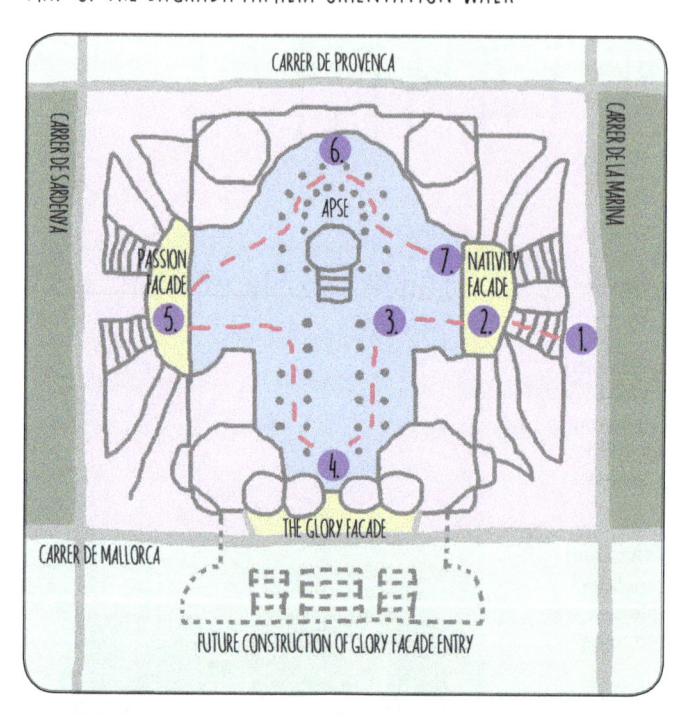

(Map showing: Carrer de Provença, Carrer de Sardenya, Carrer de la Marina, Carrer de Mallorca; locations marked 1–7; APSE, PASSION FACADE (5), NATIVITY FACADE (2), THE GLORY FACADE (4), FUTURE CONSTRUCTION OF GLORY FACADE ENTRY)

1. INSIDE THE ENTRY GATE

Enter the Sagrada Familia grounds through the ticket entry on Carrer de la Marina. Stop once inside the gates to start your orientation walk.

"Antoni Gaudi designed the Sagrada Familia. Construction started in 1882 and it is still being built today. It is expected to be finished in 2026.

Gaudi wanted to design a church that would impact on the skyline of Barcelona. When it is finished, the building will be 172 metres tall. It will be one of the tallest structures in Barcelona and it will have 18 towers."

---

* FYI

An 'orientation walk' is a first look around to get yourself familiar with a place.

A 'facade' is the outside wall of a building, usually the main wall that faces the street.

2 NATIVITY FACADE

Walk up the stairs towards the Nativity Facade*.

💬

"Construction on the eastern facade was started in 1892, while Gaudi was still alive. It is known as the 'Nativity facade' and it shows the story of the birth of Jesus Christ."

3 INSIDE THE CHURCH

Enter the church and walk forward into the main space to take a good look around.

💬

"Over 40 columns support the roof structure. Each column has a double twist. Gaudi wanted the columns to look like a forest of tree trunks. The branches at the top spread out to support the roof."

4 BACK OF THE CHURCH

Turn left and walk towards the back of the church. Stop at the back to look down the whole length of the church.

💬

"Gaudi based his design ideas on nature. He did not design using straight lines or flat surfaces, as they do not appear in the natural world."

5 PASSION FACADE

Walk up the other side of the church to the doors opposite to where you came in. Walk outside and look at the sculptures around the entrance.

💬

"This side of the church is known as the 'Passion facade' and it tells the story of Jesus Christ's death and resurrection."

6 THE APSE

Step back into the church and walk to the apse.

💬

"Gaudi believed that 'colour was the expression of life'. We can see that belief in the colourful designs of the stained glass windows."

7 BACK TO THE ENTRY

Walk back towards the door you entered by.

💬

"With the design of this church, Gaudi wanted to show his respect for God. Gaudi worked on the church for 43 years. He is buried in the crypt of the Sagrada Familia."

That is the end of the orientation walk.

SAGRADA FAMILIA MEANS 'SACRED FAMILY' IN SPANISH

SCAVENGER HUNT

ACTIVITY 22. @ SAGRADA FAMILIA

👁 CAN YOU SPOT THESE TWENTY-ONE THINGS AROUND THE CHURCH?

ON THE NATIVITY FACADE

This star (which is the star of Bethlehem)

This donkey (which is carrying Mary and Jesus to Egypt)

This box being held by one of the Magi (the three wise men)

The name 'Maria' (which is the name 'Mary' in Spanish)

This basket

ON THE PASSION FACADE

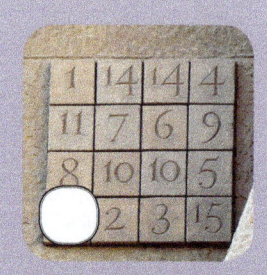

The 'magic square' where every column and row adds up to 33 – the age Jesus is believed to have been when he died. Can you work out what number is in the bottom left square?

The name 'Jesus' on the right side Gospel door

This alpha and omega symbol

This sword digging into rock

INSIDE AND OUTSIDE AROUND THE CHURCH

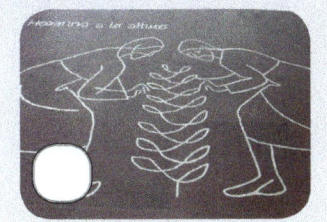

This floor etching

These snail sculptures

This plaque about the Pope's consecration of the church in 2010

These leaves and bugs (hint: on the Door of Charity)

The emblem of St Luke

This Papal coat of arms sculpture

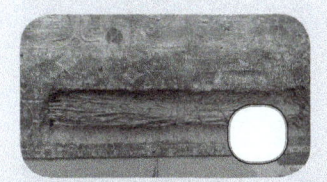

This detail on a door (hint: on the Door of the Crown of Thorns)

A turtle at the base of a column

IN THE MUSEUM UNDER THE CHURCH

This illustration of the Passion Facade by sculptor Josep Maria Subirachs

This model showing how Gaudi designed catenary arches

This model of the Passion Facade

This candelabra

THE STAINED GLASS WINDOWS

ABOUT THE STAINED GLASS WINDOWS

The colourful lead-light windows are a beautiful feature of the church. Have a look at how the colours are arranged – reds, oranges and yellows arranged together, gradually shifting to greens and blues.

Spanish artist Joan Vila i Grau was commissioned to design the windows for the church in 1999. He has followed Gaudi's ideas, which described how the church should be bathed in light and the arrangement of colour should draw your eye upwards.

WINDOW HUNT

Can you find this window inside the church? If you get stuck, read this hint. (If you don't want the hint, stop reading now. Hint: look on the inside of the Nativity Facade.)

UNDER CONSTRUCTION: THE GLORY FACADE AND SPIRES

The Glory Facade, facing Carrer de Mallorca, is still being worked on. It will be the main entry to the church. For it to be completed as planned, the complete block of buildings over the road will need to be demolished.

The church will have 18 spires when it is finished. The central, tallest spire will be 172 metres tall. The height was intended to be less than the height of Montjuic Hill as Gaudi thought the work of man shouldn't surpass the work of God. When the central spire is built, the Sagrada Familia will be the tallest church building in the world.

DRAW STAINED GLASS WINDOWS

ACTIVITY 23. @ SAGRADA FAMILIA

DRAW YOUR FAVOURITE STAINED GLASS WINDOW

Choose your favourite window. Now, take a seat and draw your own picture of the window.

First, draw the outline shape of the window. Then draw the black lead lines separating the different glass pieces. Finally colour it in, trying to copy the original flow of colours – reds to oranges to greens to blues.

BUILDING THE SAGRADA FAMILIA

THE BEGINNINGS

1874   A religious group in Barcelona began campaigning for a new church

1881   They purchased land for the church

1882   Construction commenced. The design of the church was drawn up by an architect who soon resigned from the job.

Construction in 1929

GAUDI'S WORK

1883   Antoni Gaudi became the Sagrada Familia's new architect.

1889   Gaudi suggested they abandon the original design and use his innovative new design with soaring towers.

GAUDI WORKED ON THE CHURCH FOR 43 YEARS

1914   Gaudi decided to work only on the Sagrada Familia.

1923   Gaudi finished the design of the church.

1925   The first bell tower on the Nativity facade was completed

1926   Gaudi died after a tram accident. He was buried in the crypt of the Sagrada Familia.

AFTER GAUDI

1926   After Gaudi's death, other architects took over the project.

1958   Nativity facade sculptures finished.

1961   The crypt museum was completed.

1976   Passion Facade bell towers completed.

2002   Construction of Glory Facade commenced.

2010   The building was consecrated as a place of worship by the Pope.

2026   Construction of the church is expected to be complete.

IF IT IS FINISHED IN 2026, THE SAGRADA FAMILIA WILL HAVE TAKEN 144 YEARS TO BUILD.

FIND GAUDI IN SCULPTURE

Josep Maria Subirachs was a Spanish artist who created the sculptures for the Passion Facade. It took him 20 years to carve the 100 stone figures and cast the four bronze doors.

He included a sculpture of Gaudi in his design to pay homage to the architect. Can you spot the Gaudi sculpture?

SAGRADA FAMILIA CROSSWORD

ACTIVITY 24. @ ANYWHERE

READ THIS CHAPTER THEN ANSWER THE CLUES

Once you have read the information about the Sagrada Familia in this chapter, you should be able to answer all of the crossword clue questions. Then fit your answers in to the crossword grid below.

THE CLUES

Who designed the Sagrada Familia? (6,5)

The name of the eastern wall (the story of Jesus's birth) is the Nativity _____ (6)

What type of information centre is housed underneath the church? (6)

Coloured glass in church windows is known as _____ glass (7)

The columns in the church are intended to look like a _____ (6)

The ticket entrance is on the street Carrer de la _____ (6)

Gaudi believed that "colour was the expression of _____" (4)

When the church is completed, it will have 18 of what? (6)

Sagrada Familia means sacred _____ (6)

The church will be 172 _____ tall when finished (6)

What city is the Sagrada Familia in? (9)

The name of the west entry (the story of Jesus's death) is the _____ facade (7)

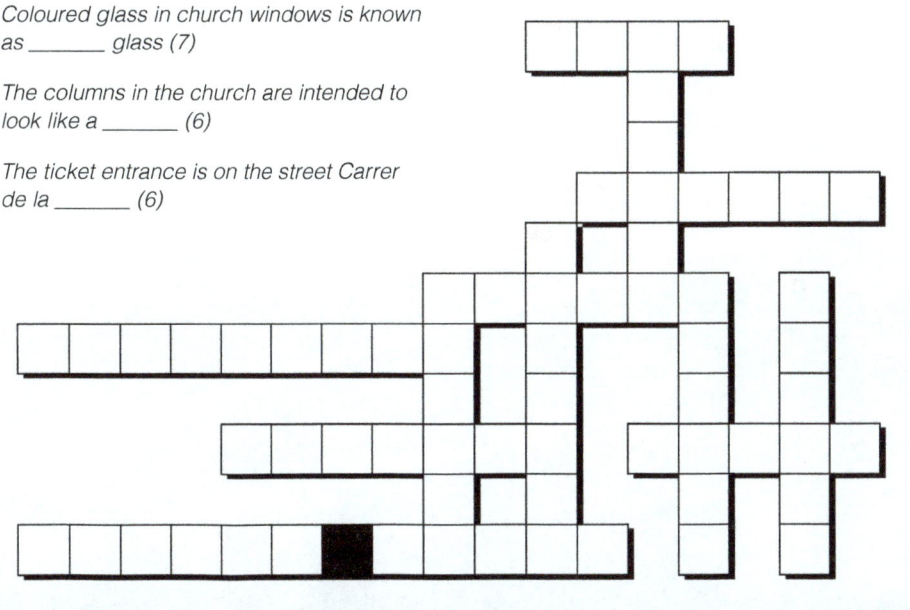

Museu Picasso

Ajuntament de Barcelona

CHAPTER 6

MUSEU PICASSO

The Museu Picasso is a museum dedicated to the work of Spanish artist Pablo Picasso. Picasso was a painter, sculptor, printmaker and ceramicist. He is one of the world's most famous and influential artists.

The Museu Picasso in Barcelona was opened in 1963. It houses one of the biggest collections of Picasso's work anywhere in the world. Picasso donated many of his artworks to the museum.

Photo, left: sign at the museum.
Above: Picasso and his sister Lola in 1889.

A QUICK LIFE STORY OF PICASSO

Picasso was born in Malaga in Spain in 1881. From early childhood, he showed a talent for painting and drawing.

When Picasso was thirteen, the family moved to Barcelona and Picasso enrolled in the School of Fine Arts. At sixteen, he went to Spain's best art school in Madrid.

Picasso continued to learn and paint. He developed different painting styles and became a very famous artist.

He spent much of his adult life in France. He created a huge amount of artwork which is on display in galleries all over the world. Picasso died in 1973 when he was 91 years old.

DRAWING WITH PERSPECTIVE

ACTIVITY 25. @ MUSEU PICASSO ROOM 2

LOOK CLOSELY AT THE PAINTING 'MAS DEL QUIQUET'

Find the painting 'Mas del Quiquet' (Quiquet's Farmhouse) in Room 2.

Picasso moved to the country for six months in 1898 when he was 17 years old. He stayed in a town called Horta D'Ebra and he painted many country scenes, including this one.

This painting shows a farm house and it uses perspective and shading to show the three dimensional house shape. You can use some of these techniques to draw your own farm house.

DRAW YOUR OWN FARMHOUSE

Take a look at the information about drawing with perspective and shading.

Then, draw your own farmhouse using the perspective grid opposite and colour it in using light and dark shades of a colour.

> PICASSO'S FULL NAME IS:
> PABLO DIEGO JOSE FRANCISCO DE PAULA JUAN NEPOMUCENO MARIA DE LOS REMEDIOS CIPRIANO DE LA SANTISIMA TRINIDAD RUIZ Y PICASSO

PERSPECTIVE

Perspective is the principle of how things look from a certain point of view. Things appear smaller the further away they are.

We can use a line framework to help us draw in perspective – that is, to draw things gradually getting smaller the further away from us they are. The lines in the framework all meet at what is called the 'vanishing point'. Here's an example of how you use the framework to draw a picture.

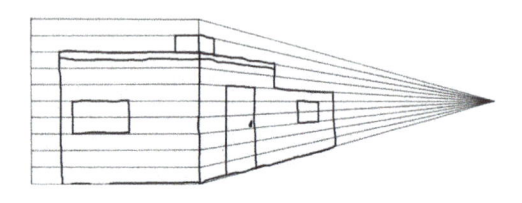

SHADING

You can use darker and lighter tones of a colour to indicate shadow and light. See how Picasso used a bright yellow for the wall facing towards us, then a darker yellow for the side wall, to give an impression of shadow. For your picture, choose a colour for your front wall. Then choose a darker tone of that colour for the side wall. Here's an example of how to use tones to shade your drawing.

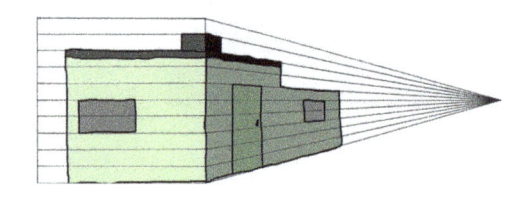

THIS WAY UP

STILL LIFE COUNT UP

ACTIVITY 26. @ MUSEU PICASSO ROOM 7

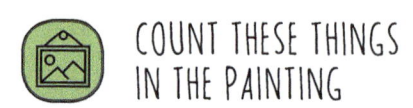

COUNT THESE THINGS IN THE PAINTING

* FYI

A 'still life' is a painting of common everyday objects - things that stay still. Artists will often arrange items like fruit, vegetables, cups and plates on a table to paint.

Find the painting Still Life (1901) in Room 7.

Look carefully at the painting and count up the things below. Then use the numbers to crack the code and answer the question.

HOW MANY ORANGES CAN YOU SEE IN THE BOWL?	HOW MANY BLUE LINES ARE ON THE HANDLE OF THE MUG?
HOW MANY YELLOW FLOWERS ARE IN THE VASE?	HOW MANY GRAPES CAN YOU COUNT?
HOW MANY FORKS ARE ON THE TABLE?	HOW MANY WHITE FLOWERS ARE IN THE VASE?

CODEBREAKER

1	2	3	4	5	6	7	9	13	18	26	30
E	S	A	T	F	Y	I	O	R	L	P	M

QUESTION: WHAT DID PICASSO HAVE FOR LUNCH THE DAY HE PAINTED THIS STILL LIFE?

ANSWER:

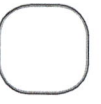

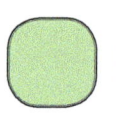

CLASSIFY THAT PICASSO

ACTIVITY 27. @ MUSEU PICASSO

PICASSO'S EARLY PAINTING PERIODS

Early in Picasso's career, from around 1901 to around 1917, he developed distinct painting styles. The different styles are described below.

From 1917 onwards, Picasso's artistic style developed and changed, but did not fall into such distinct periods.

WHICH PERIOD IS THIS PAINTING FROM?

As you walk through the gallery – especially rooms 8 and 9 – try to spot paintings that belong to each period. (Tip: check the date the artwork was created to help you.)

If you think you can classify a painting to a period, put a tick next to that period. Tally up how many paintings of each style you identify.

BLUE PERIOD (1901-1904)

Sombre (serious and sad) paintings mainly painted in shades of blue and bluey-green (sometimes showing poor people or old people).

ROSE PERIOD (1904 - 1906)

More cheery and optimistic paintings often using shades of red and orange (some showing circus performers).

AFRICAN-INFLUENCED PERIOD (1907 - 1909)

A style influenced by African art. These artworks sometimes have black outlines and angular shapes. (These paintings were radical and not very well liked.)

CUBISM (1909 - 1912)

A style developed with Georges Braque, mainly using brown and neutral tones. The artists analysed the shapes of the things they were painting, rather than trying to paint what things look like.

CRYSTAL PERIOD (1912 - 1917)

A development of the cubist style, showing objects in a very geometric way, with angular lines and shapes making up the form of the image.

THERE ARE OVER 3500 ARTWORKS BY PICASSO IN THE PERMANENT COLLECTION OF THE MUSEUM

SPOT THE DIFFERENCE

ACTIVITY 28. @ MUSEU PICASSO ROOM 12

PICASSO'S LAS MENINAS SERIES

Find the painting Las Meninas (group) in Room 12.

Las Meninas (group) and Las Meninas (infanta Margarita Maria) are two of the many paintings that Picasso did in a series of works based on another painting.

The painting they were based on is pictured here – it is called 'Las Meninas' by the artist Diego Velazquez. (Velazquez's painting is in Museo del Prado in Madrid – make sure you check it out if you go to the Prado.)

Compare Valazquez's painting to Picasso's painting. Can you see how the two paintings are of the same thing and yet very different?

SPOT THE DIFFERENCE

The paintings are very different, but you can see that Picasso's painting is based on Valazquez's painting.

Can you spot six things in Picasso's painting that are the same – but different – from Velazquez's painting?

WHAT IS THE SAME AS VELAZQUEZ'S PAINTING?

eg. a person in doorway

HOW IS IT DIFFERENT IN PICASSO'S PAINTING?

looks like a triangle shape

DRAW A PICASSO-STYLE PORTRAIT

ACTIVITY 29. @ MUSEU PICASSO ROOM 13

LOOK AT THE PORTRAIT OF INFANTA MARGARITA MARIA

Find the painting Las Meninas (infanta Margarita Maria) (1957) in Room 13.

Take a good look at it. Can you see the way her face is painted – the eyes are not the same, the triangle of the nose is shown side on, while two nostrils seem to face the front. Look at the way shapes are used – the box of her skirt, the kite shape of her sleeve, the round curve of her cheek, the shapes in her hair.

DRAW YOUR OWN PORTRAIT

Have a go at drawing your own Picasso-style portrait. Draw a person – but the rule is that you can only use shapes. You can't use any lines that are not enclosing a shape.

Put your shapes next to each other or overlapping. Then use coloured pencils to colour in the different shapes of your portrait.

PIGEON MATHEMATICS

ACTIVITY 30. @ MUSEU PICASSO ROOM 15

COUNT THE PIGEONS AND DO THE MATHS TO WORK OUT PICASSO'S AGE

Find the work 'The Pigeons' in Room 15.

In the middle of painting his Las Meninas series, Picasso took a week's break and painted nine paintings of the view out of his window.

All nine paintings feature pigeons and are in a very different style from the Las Meninas series. The pigeon paintings are colourful and lively.

Count the pigeons and do the sums to find the two digits that make up Picasso's age.

How many pigeons are on the left, surrounded by black lines?

plus +

How many pigeons are sitting on the ground at the bottom of the painting?

=

HOW OLD WAS PICASSO WHEN HE PAINTED THIS PAINTING?

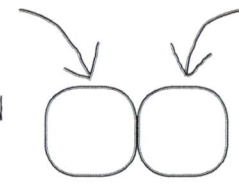

How many pigeons can you count in the picture altogether?

divided by ÷

How many pigeons are sitting on the trellis fence?

=

THE FIVE PALACES OF THE PICASSO MUSEUM

The Picasso Museum building was not always one building.

The museum is housed inside what used to be five buildings. The five buildings were palaces – important houses built between the 13th and 15th centuries.

When the Museu Picasso opened in 1963, it was in one of the buildings. The next building was added in 1970, with renovation works to connect them together. Another palace was added to the museum in 1982. Two more were added in 1999 to form the museum that you visit today.

PICASSO SHORT STORY

ACTIVITY 31. @ MUSEU PICASSO (OR ANYWHERE)

WRITE A 100-WORD STORY BASED ON A PICASSO ARTWORK

Choose an artwork in the Picasso Museum. This will be the basis for your story.

You could imagine that you are in the artwork – what do you think is happening? You could imagine that you were the artist – what was happening while you created this artwork? Or you can simply use the artwork for a starting your idea for a story.

The story should be short – about 100 words long. If you want a challenge, make the story EXACTLY 100 words.

If you need an idea, here's a first line:

"The moment I saw the artwork, I could tell that… "

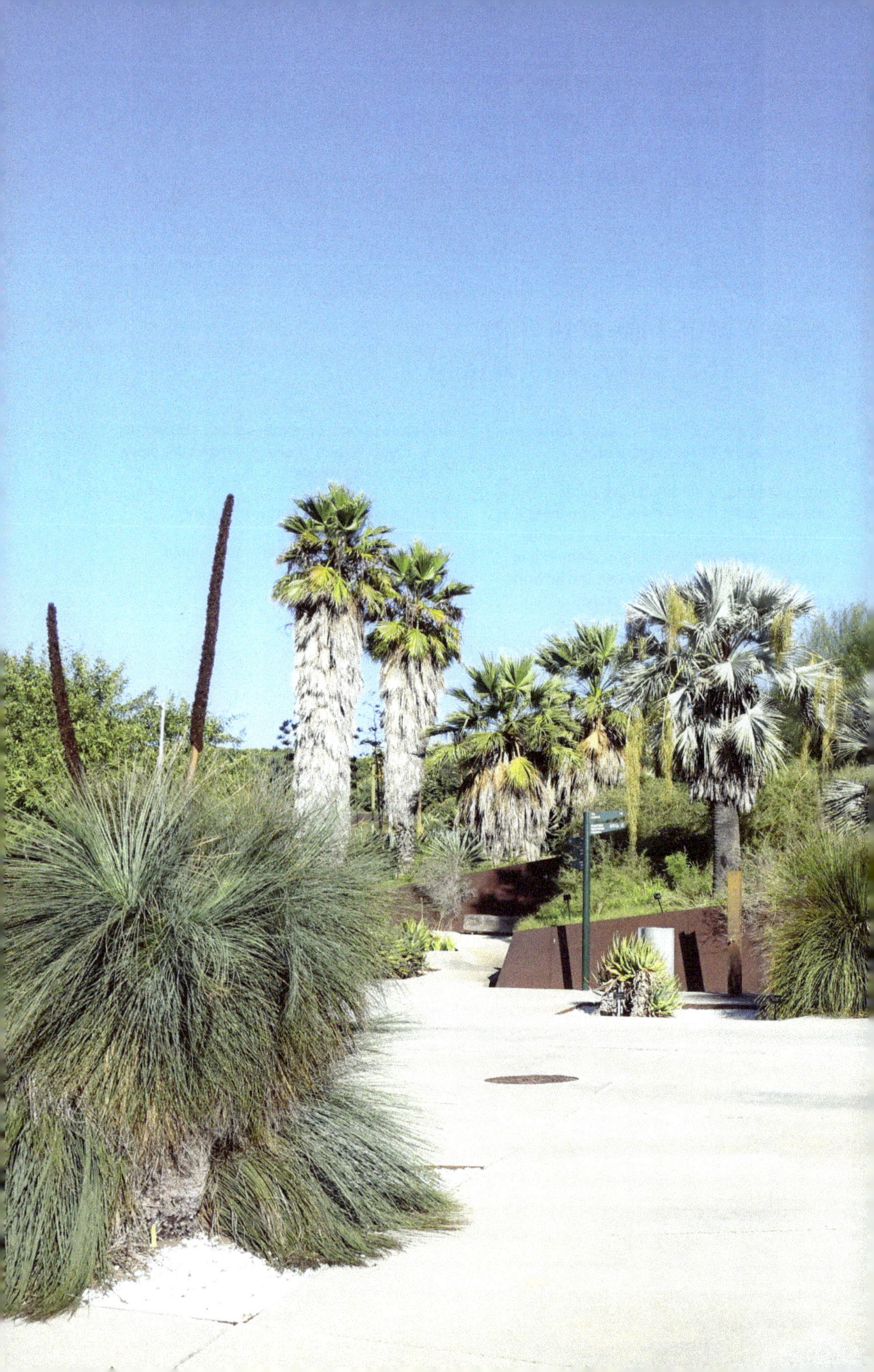

CHAPTER 7

MONTJUIC HILL

Montjuic is an area of Barcelona that holds the city's highest point – Montjuic Hill. Montjuic has great views across the city and a ton of parkland, making it a perfect place for a sunny day outdoors.

Two big events in history have had an impact on Montjuic – the 1929 International Exposition and the 1992 Olympic Games.

Both of these events were an opportunity for Barcelona to show itself to the world. Many new construction projects were completed to prepare for the events.

*Photo, left: The Jardi Botanic.
Right: a poster for the
1929 International Exposition.*

1929 INTERNATIONAL EXPOSITION

Barcelona re-vamped the Montjuic area to be the centre of the 1929 Exposition. The main show-pieces built for the Exposition were the Palau Nacional, the Magic Fountain, Placa Espanya, Teatre Grec and Poble Espanyol.

1992 SUMMER OLYMPIC GAMES

Barcelona did another re-vamp to prepare itself for the world's attention during the 1992 Olympic Games. The stadium built for the 1929 Exposition was fixed up to become the main Olympic Stadium. The Olympic Park area of Montjuic contains the stadium, swimming pools, athletics tracks and other venues. The telecommunications tower is an iconic sight in the area.

BARCELONA VIEW FINDER

ACTIVITY 32. @ PALAU NACIONAL

THE PALAU NACIONAL

The Palau Nacional building is set on Montjuic Hill. The ornate palace was built to be the centrepiece of the 1929 International Exposition.

Today the building houses a museum – the Museu Nacional D'Art de Catalunya. There are over 5000 artworks in the museum collection.

Climb the stairs to the terrace outside the Palau Nacional for great views across Barcelona. If you go into the museum, head up to the rooftop terrace for even better views.

SO MANY STAIRS

If you walk up the stairs from the Magic Fountain to the Palau Nacional, count the stairs as you go.

How many stairs did you count?

CAN YOU SPOT THESE BARCELONA LANDMARKS?

From your highest viewpoint, see if you can spot:

- The Magic Fountain – at the foot of the stairs leading up to the Palau Nacional

- The Venetian Towers – the two red towers that were built to mark the entrance to the 1929 Exposition area

- Placa Espanya – the grassy plaza in the middle of the big roundabout behind the Venetian Towers

- Arenas de Barcelona – the round building next to Placa Espanya (it was a bullring, now it's a shopping centre)

- Torre Glories – this 38 story round tower opened in 2005 to mark the entry to Barcelona's tech district

- The Sagrada Familia – Gaudi's church will be almost as tall as Montjuic Hill when it is finished

- The tower on Tibidabo Mountain – a communications tower that sits on the highest peak in Barcelona

- Sagrat Cor church on Tibidabo Mountain – see if you can spot the amusement park next to the church too

MAGIC FOUNTAIN NUMBER PUZZLE

ACTIVITY 33. @ ANYWHERE

THE MAGIC FOUNTAIN OF MONTJUIC

The Magic Fountain of Montjuic was designed and constructed for the 1929 Barcelona International Exposition.

A night-time visit to see the Magic Fountain is a lot of fun. The fountain is lit up with a colourful light show and it sprays water in time to music.

CAN YOU FILL IN THE MISSING NUMBERS?

In this puzzle, each number on the Magic Fountain is the sum of the two numbers below. Fill in the numbers that are missing to complete the Magic Fountain.

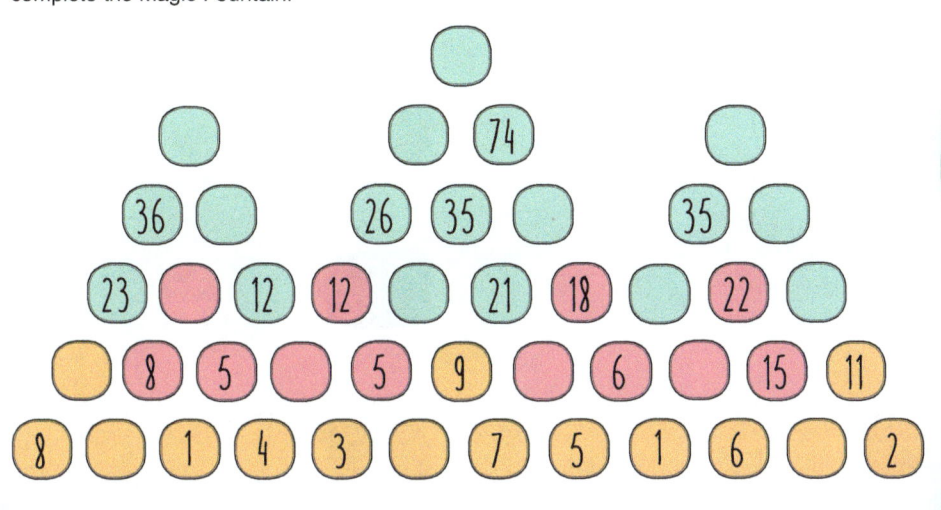

Row 1: 74

Row 2: 26, 35

Row 3: 36, 35

Row 4: 23, 12, 12, 21, 18, 22

Row 5: 8, 5, 5, 9, 6, 15, 11

Row 6: 8, 1, 4, 3, 7, 5, 1, 6, 2

PARKLAND COLOUR HUNT

ACTIVITY 34. @ A PARK IN MONTJUIC (OR ANY PARK)

FIND THESE COLOURS IN THE PARK

Each season the colours in the parks will change, as different plants come into flower, berries grow and leaves change colour.

Go on a colour hunt to find a whole rainbow of colours within the park to match this colour chart. Find a colour in the park and hold the book up next to it to see if the colour matches. When you have found a colour match, write down what is was or draw a quick sketch of it.

Remember, you are in a public parkland – don't pick leaves, flowers, seeds, grasses or anything from the growing plants and don't walk in the garden beds.

PARKLAND NATURE BINGO

ACTIVITY 35. @ A PARK IN MONTJUIC (OR ANY PARK)

SPOT THESE THINGS IN THE PARK

Try to spot these things in the park. When you have got four things in a row, it's bingo! Once you have got bingo, try to spot everything on the bingo card for double bingo.

THE PORT CABLE CAR

Barcelona has two cable cars that connect to Montjuic (see Chapter 9 for details of their routes). The Port Cable Car has incredible views, but be warned – it's for brave passengers only.

A PERSON CARRYING A BAG	A WORM	A LARGE STONE	A RUBBISH BIN
A BUG OR BEETLE	A CURVING PATH	A BIRD	A PURPLE FLOWER
A PALM TREE	SOMETHING MADE OF GLASS	A SIGNPOST	A BUTTERFLY
A DOG	AN ANT	A CACTUS	A SEAT

MORE ABOUT MONTJUIC

JEAN MIRO - SPANISH ARTIST

Jean Miro was a Spanish artist born in Barcelona in 1893. He grew up in the Barri Gotic neighbourhood and began drawing classes at the age of seven. He later enrolled in art college and had his first solo art show at the age of 24. In 1919 he travelled to Paris and became friends with many artists including Picasso.

Miro experimented with his art and developed his own individual style, recognisable for its distinctive use of colour, shape and line. Over his life, he created paintings, sculptures, ceramics, mosaics, murals and illustrated books.

You may have seen some of Miro's work in Barcelona – there's the Pla de L'Os mosaic on La Rambla, the huge Woman and Bird statue in Parc de Joan Miro and the wall mosaic at Barcelona airport (pictured above).

MIRO'S GALLERY

Fundacio Joan Miro is a gallery in Montjuic dedicated to Miro's work. If you go to the gallery, you'll see lots of Miro's artwork – plus one of the few liquid mercury fountains in the world.

MEASURING THE FIRST METRE AT MONTJUIC CASTLE

In 1794, two astronomers measured the distance around the curve of the earth between a high point in Dunkirk in the UK and Barcelona's high point, the fortress on Montjuic Hill.

From the measurement they took, they calculated the distance between the North Pole and the Equator.

From that distance, they created the metre – one ten millionth of the distance between the North Pole and the Equator.

DRAW A MIRO-STYLE PICTURE

ACTIVITY 36. @ ANYWHERE

DRAW YOUR OWN MIRO-STYLE PICTURE

Get out a black pencil or pen. Re-draw each of these ten lines and shapes, but draw them in different sizes and directions and crossing over each other.

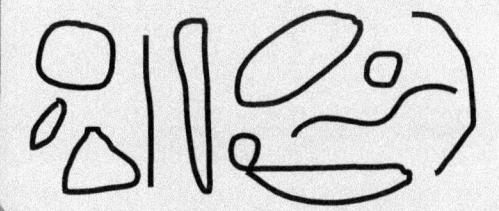

Next get out only these pencils:

bright blue   bright green
bright red   light grey
bright yellow black

Now colour in your picture using one strong colour for each area or shape – don't blend colours or use colours lightly. Fill in the whole box – but you can leave sections in plain white if you wish. And there you have it – your own Miro-style artwork.

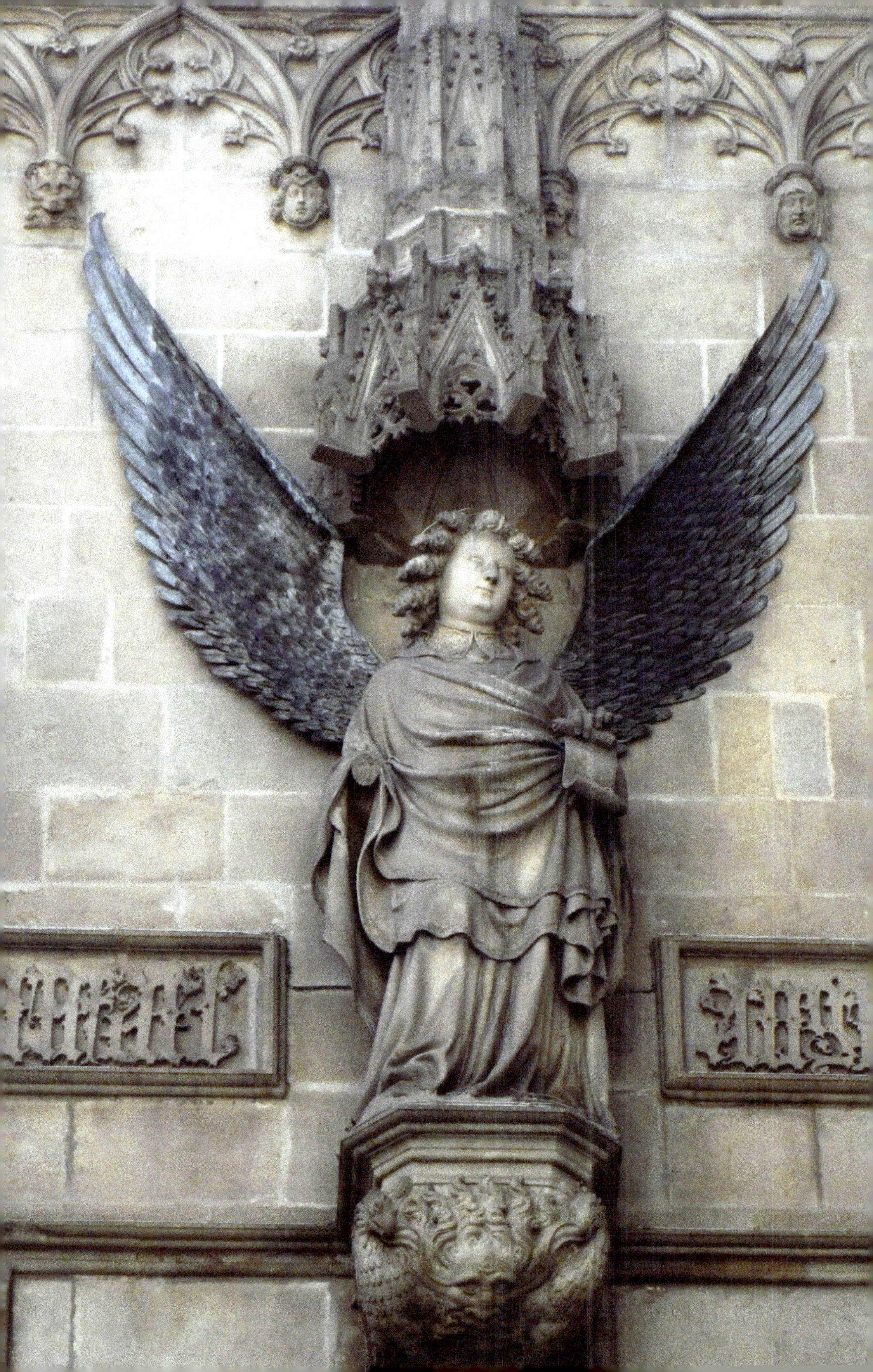

CHAPTER 8

ACROSS BARCELONA

This chapter contains activities that you can do across Barcelona.

Some are for doing all the time – like looking out for things that are in different places across the city.

And some can be done at any time – whenever you feel like doing an activity.

This chapter also has some information about some of the churches you might see around Barcelona. If you spot a church, see if you can find it in this chapter and tick it off.

CHURCH OF SANTA MARIA DEL MAR

This imposing Gothic church in the Ribera district of the Old Town was built between 1329 and 1383. The church has had its share of bad luck – an earthquake in 1428 destroyed the rose window at the west end (it was replaced in 1459) and a fire in 1936 destroyed much of the decoration inside the church.

Photo, left: A sculpture of Sant Raphael on a building in the Old Town.
Right: Church of Santa Maria del Mar.

SPOT THAT SHAPE

ACTIVITY 37. @ ACROSS BARCELONA

FIND THESE SHAPES AROUND THE CITY

As you explore Barcelona, you'll see different kinds of shapes – perhaps a square window, a round clock or a triangle street sign.

Fill in these shapes with drawings of things of same shape that you spot around Barcelona.

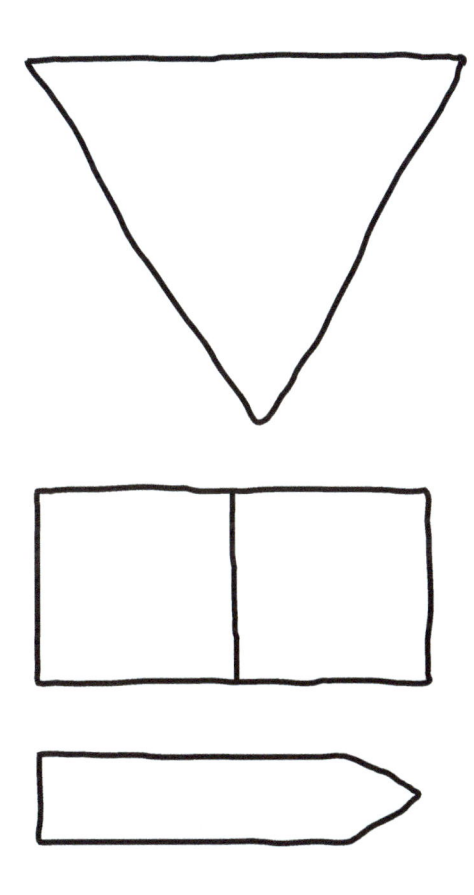

COMPLETE THIS SQUIGGLE

Turn this squiggle into a picture of something you have seen in Barcelona.

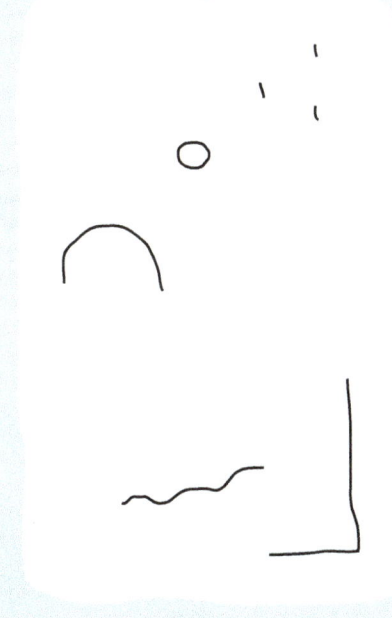

SANTA MARIA DEL PI STATISTICS

Santa Maria del Pi is a church in the Barri Gotic area. It was built between 1319 and 1391. The church features a bell tower which is 54 metres tall. The length of the nave inside the church is also 54 metres.

At the base of the bell tower, the walls are incredibly thick – over 3.5 metres thick. There are six bells in the tower and the largest bell is 1.4 metres wide.

Inside the church are four of the giant puppets that are used to celebrate festivals in Catalonia.

ENERGY BURN CHALLENGE

ACTIVITY 38. @ IN A PARK

FIRST, SET UP A TEN METRE TRACK FOR THE CHALLENGE

Head to a park or any open space and create a ten-metre track. Find two markers that are about ten metres apart – perhaps trees or statues or just put sticks on the ground. Choose one end of the track to be your start line.

Ask someone in your group to set a timer or stopwatch. You have six minutes to complete all the exercises in this list.

No cheating! Lift your legs and arms up high!

TWO MINUTE CHALLENGE

Put a timer on for two minutes. Run on the spot and count your steps as you run – see if you can get two hundred steps in two minutes.

BASILICA DE LA MERCE

The Basilica de la Merce is a church in the Barri Gotic area. It is well-known for the statue of Mary on the top – if you look carefully, you might be able to see the statue from the waterfront.

THE ENERGY BURN CHALLENGE

At start line. Stopwatch ready. Ready, set, go!

1. Do 30 star jumps.
2. Run to your end marker and back six times.
3. Raise your arms and jump as high as you can in the air then squat down and touch the ground. Repeat ten times.
4. Hop to your end marker. Then skip back. Repeat four times.
5. Run on the spot with high knees, tapping your knees with your hands. Count out 30 high knee taps.
6. Do baby steps to your end marker (placing the heel of one foot touching the toe of the other foot) and jump back. Repeat one more time.
7. Do twenty squats with arms stretched out in front.
8. Run to your end marker and back six times.

STOP!

DID YOU DO IT IN SIX MINUTES?

IF YOU DID, TRY TO DO IT IN FIVE MINUTES NEXT TIME.

FONT MASTER

ACTIVITY 39. @ ANYWHERE

abc — WRITE THESE WORDS IN DIFFERENT FONTS

Write these words in five different fonts each. Make your fonts as crazy or colourful as you like.

>>> TREES IN A ROW

A gardener wanted to plant five rows of four trees, but she only had ten trees. She worked out a way to do it. Can you work out how?

BARCELONA

SPAIN

GAUDI

SPANISH

PICASSO

TAPAS

PUBLIC ART TREASURE HUNT

ACTIVITY 40. @ ACROSS BARCELONA

KEEP A LOOK OUT FOR THESE ARTWORKS

See if you can spot these public artworks while you are out and about on the streets of Barcelona. Tick them off as you spot them.

MANY OF THESE ARTWORKS WERE COMMISSIONED FOR THE 1992 OLYMPIC GAMES

PICASSO FRIEZES

ARTISTS
Pablo Picasso and Carl Nesjar

WHERE
College of Architects building, Placa Nova, Barri Gotic

ABOUT
An artwork by Pablo Picasso has been made into three large public friezes on the College of Architects building by sculptor Carl Nesjar.

BARCELONA FACE

ARTIST
Roy Lichtenstein

WHERE
At the intersection of Passeig de Colom and Via Laietana, near the waterfront

ABOUT
This sculpture, commissioned for the 1992 Olympic Games, was inspired by Gaudi. It uses Lichtenstein's classic comic book style and colours in a three dimensional form.

THE FISH

ARTIST
Frank Gehry

WHERE
At the waterfront near the end of Carrer de la Marina

ABOUT
This giant gold fish sculpture overlooks Barceloneta beach. It's 56 metres long and 35 metres high.

WOMAN AND BIRD

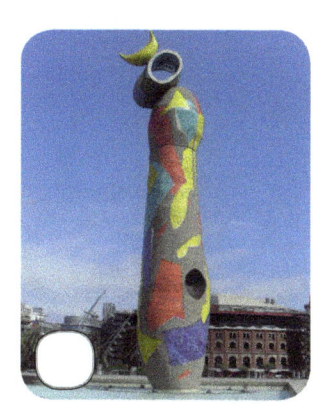

ARTISTS

Jean Miro
with Joan Gardy Artigas

WHERE

Park de Joan Miro,
near Placa D'Espanya

ABOUT

This 22 metre high sculpture was one of three artworks that Miro created to welcome visitors to Barcelona.
(The others are the mosaic at La Rambla and the mural at the airport.)

RAVAL CAT

ARTIST

Fernando Botero

WHERE

At the bottom of Rambla del Raval

ABOUT

This fat cat was relocated to a few different spots in Barcelona – including Parc de la Ciutadella and Montjuic – before it settled into Rambla del Raval. He has settled in now and is a much loved part of the neighbourhood.

WOUNDED FALLING STAR

ARTIST

Rebecca Horn

WHERE

Barceloneta beach

ABOUT

Four cubes with windows stacked crookedly on top of each other are said to represent the old fishermen's shacks of Barceloneta or the ramshackle beach-front cafes that were here before the revamp of the area for the 1992 Olympics.

GAMBRINUS

ARTIST

Javier Mariscal

WHERE

The waterfront, not far from the end of Via Laietana

ABOUT

This giant prawn once belonged to a restaurant called Gambrinus. The restaurant closed long ago but the statue remains a much loved icon on the waterfront.

ACTIVITY 40: PUBLIC ART TREASURE HUNT – CONTINUED

THINKING BULL

ARTIST

Josep Granyer

WHERE

Rambla de Catalunya, at the intersection with Gran Via

ABOUT

Created in 1972, this small statue of a bull sitting and thinking is a local favourite. The pose of this statue is similar to a famous statue in Paris – The Thinker by Auguste Rodin.

STARGAZERS

ARTIST

Robert Llimos

WHERE

On the water just off Rambla de Mar – which is near the end of La Rambla.

ABOUT

The two figures are afloat in the water – each figure stands with legs wide apart, looks up at the sky and holds a coloured star behind its back.

HOMAGE TO SWIMMING

ARTIST

Alfredo Lanz

WHERE

Placa del Mar, at Sant Sebastia Beach

ABOUT

This Olympic-inspired sculpture represents the sports of swimming, diving, water polo and synchronised swimming amongst water and waves. Can you see where the different sports are represented in the statue?

BARCINO

ARTIST

Joan Brossa

WHERE

Placa Nova, Barri Gotic

ABOUT

Spelling out the name of the old Roman colony, this artwork sits near the Roman wall. Six of the letters are made of bronze and the 'N' is made of aluminium. Each letter is its own individual work of art – the 'N' looks like a sailboat, the 'C' is a moon, and the 'O' is a sun.

WORDS FROM BARCELONA

ACTIVITY 41. @ ANYWHERE

HOW MANY WORDS CAN YOU MAKE FROM ONE WORD?

How many words can you make out of the letters in the word 'Barcelona'?

For example, you can make the words 'coal' and 'crab' using the letters.

Each letter can only be used once per word. Write down as many words as you can.

B A R
C E L
O N A

SCORE

Less than 10 words:
Good job

11 – 20 words:
Great job

21 – 39 words:
Brilliant work

over 40 words:
You are amazing

TAPAS TIME

ACTIVITY 42. @ EATING OUT

WHAT ARE THESE SPANISH DISHES?

Find out what these dishes are and describe them. If you have ordered them at a restaurant, rate the dish out of ten (where 1 = not very nice and 10 = absolutely delicious).

RATING

PATATAS BRAVAS _____ / 10

CHIPIRONES _____ / 10

CROQUETAS _____ / 10

PAN CON TOMATE _____ / 10

JAMON IBERICO _____ / 10

TORTILLA DE PATATA _____ / 10

GAMBITAS AL AJILLO _____ / 10

FIND CAMP NOU MAZE

ACTIVITY 43. @ ANYWHERE

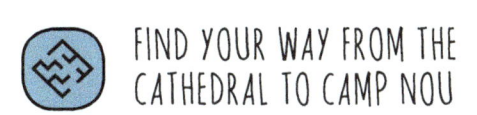

FIND YOUR WAY FROM THE CATHEDRAL TO CAMP NOU

CATHEDRAL

CAMP NOU

DRAW A BARCELONA BUILDING

ACTIVITY 44. @ OUT ON THE STREET

USE PERSPECTIVE

This might be a good activity to do when you are sitting outside at a restaurant or cafe.

Remember the perspective technique that you learnt at Museu Picasso? Below is a similar perspective grid, but with two vanishing points instead of one. An example of how to use it is drawn below right.

Find a building that you like somewhere in Barcelona. Take a seat and draw that building in the perspective grid. Then shade it using tones of one colour to create depth.

TEMPLE EXPIATORI DEL SAGRAT COR

The Temple Expiatori del Sagrat Cor is on top of Mount Tibidabo, the mountain that overlooks the city of Barcelona.

The church was designed by Spanish architect Enric Sagnier and was built between 1902 and 1961. You can see the church from many viewpoints in Barcelona.

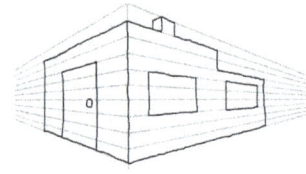

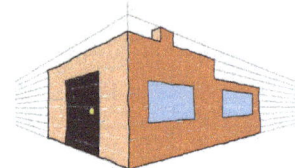

FIND ONE HUNDRED

ACTIVITY 45. @ OUT ON THE STREET

☑ COUNT TO 100

Each time you see a person in a hat, tick a box. See if you can find 100 people in hats.

Each time you see a person on a motorbike, tick a box. See if you can find 100 people on motorbikes.

Which did you see more of – people in hats or on motorbikes?

>>> MINI SUDOKU

Fill in the numbers 1 to 9 so that every column and row equals 15.

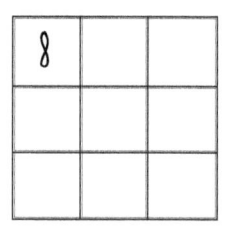

8		

PERSON WEARING A HAT

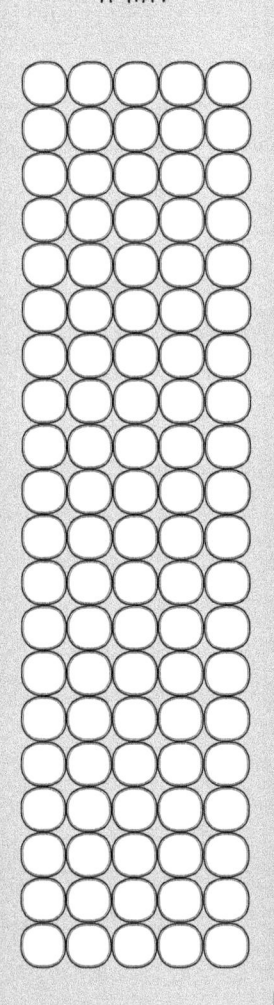

TOTAL

PERSON ON A MOTORBIKE

TOTAL

BARCELONA ALPHABET

ACTIVITY 46. @ ANYWHERE

THINK OF SOMETHING FOR EVERY LETTER

Write down something about Barcelona for every letter of the alphabet.

For example: A = awesome, B = Batllo...

>>> PET PUZZLE

I have more than two pets at home.
All of them are cats except two.
All of them are rabbits except two.
All of them are parakeets except two.
How many pets do I have
(and what are they)?

A
B
C
D
E
F
G
H
I
J
K
L
M

N
O
P
Q
R
S
T
U
V
W
X
Y
Z

HOTEL OLYMPICS

ACTIVITY 47. @ AT YOUR ACCOMMODATION

MAKE AN OLYMPIC CIRCUIT IN YOUR ROOM

Make your own Barcelona 1992 Olympic sports circuit in your hotel or accommodation. Here are four events to start you off.

1. SUPERMAN HOLD

Stand on one leg and bend over at the waist. Put your other leg straight out behind you and your arms forward (as if you are flying like superman except with one leg on the ground).

Now, hold that pose and count slowly to sixty. Can you last the whole superman minute?

2. CUP TOSS

Get a piece of paper and scrunch it into a small ball. Get a cup and place it on the floor. Step about two metres back from the cup and try to throw the ball into the cup.

Throw the ball ten times and count how many times you land the ball in the cup.

3. TRIANGLE HEAD STAND

Put a cushion on the floor. Kneel down and place your two hands flat on the floor between you and the cushion. Now, put the top of your head down on the cushion. Can you put your knees on top of your upper arms to do a triangle head stand? See if you can hold it for twenty seconds.

4. SOCK ISLANDS

Get out some socks and other small items of clothing. Place each one on the floor leaving at least a metre between them, scattered around the room.

Now, imagine the socks are islands to jump between without touching the floor.

Can you make it from a comfortable chair to the kitchen kettle not touching the floor?

Can you make it from the front door to the television?

Can you make it from your bed to the bathroom door?

Make up your own island circuits around your room.

SANT PAU DEL CAMP

The quiet haven of Sant Pau del Camp is one of the oldest surviving churches in Barcelona. The church was here before the year 911, so it's over 1100 years old.

The name of the church means 'Saint Paul of the Countryside'. It is located in the El Raval district of the city, but back in the 900s El Raval was outside the city boundary.

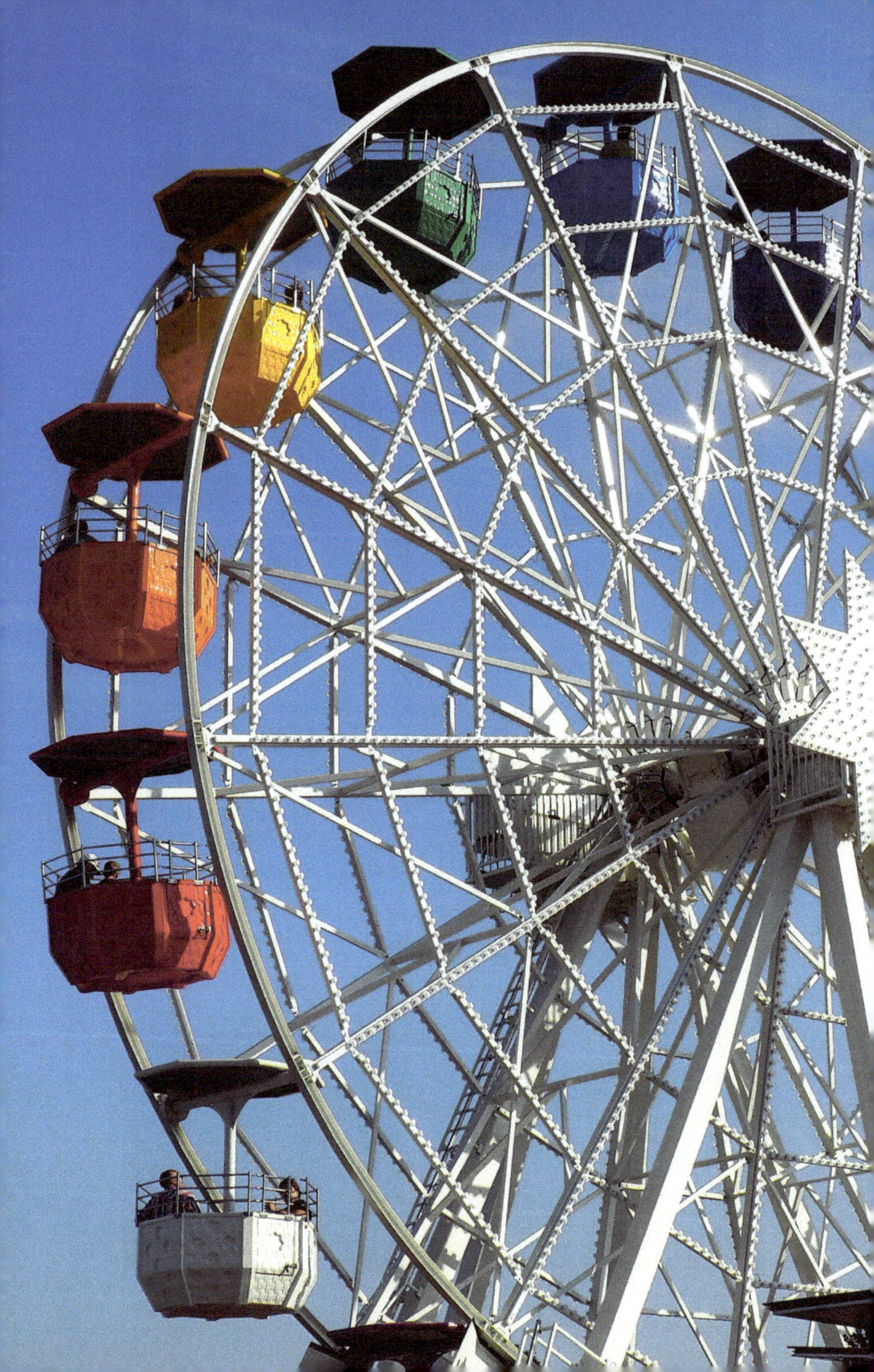

CHAPTER 9

BARCELONA FOR KIDS

This book contains activities to do in a lot of different places that you might visit in Barcelona.

But this chapter is about the places that you'll love without any extra activities. Places like museums, beaches, parks and castles.

CAMP NOU – HOME OF FC BARCELONA

Camp Nou is the home ground for the famous FC Barcelona football club. Camp Nou is the largest football stadium in Europe – it seats 99,354 people. The stadium is one of Barcelona's most visited attractions. You can visit the museum or take a stadium tour that visits the field, stands, change-rooms and commentary boxes.

Photo, left: the ferris wheel at Tibidabo Amusement Park. Above: an Indian peafowl at Barcelona zoo. Right: Camp Nou.

PARKS AND OUTDOOR SPACES

JARDIN DE JOAN BROSSA

Jardin de Joan Brossa is one of the parks in the Montjuic hill area. It has a forest, an adventure playground, a rope course, statues and fun music installations. The park, which is on the site of a former amusement park, is named after Catalan poet Joan Brossa.

JARDI BOTANIC

Barcelona's Botanic Gardens in Montjuic has beautiful views across the city. There are over 1500 different species of plant here and the park displays typical plants from six different regions of the world.

PARC DE JOAN MIRO

The playground at Parc de Joan Miro includes climbing structures, a giant swing, basketball courts and ping pong tables. Miro's giant statue, Woman and Bird, looms over the park.

JARDINS DE JOAN MARAGALL

Another park in the Montjuic hill area, the Jardins de Joan Maragall is a lovely quiet garden with fountains, statues and flowers set by a palace – the Palauet Albeniz.

PARC DE LA DIAGONAL MAR

Sweeping, looping metal structures make the modern Parc de la Diagonal Mar a great place to explore. There are play areas, a hill with slides, wooden bridges, lakes and spraying water.

PARKS IN THIS BOOK

Two great parks are covered elsewhere in this book: Parc de la Ciutadella (Activity 5) and Park Guell (Activities 19 and 20). There are also three activities that can be done at any park: Activities 34, 35 and 38.

PARC DEL LABERINT D'HORTA

The Parc del Laberint D'Horta is a quiet historical garden in the Horta-Guinado district. There are fountains, pavilions, pools and statues – the highlight is the hedge maze (or labyrinth) that the park is named for.

Water, Wildlife and Other Stuff

Beaches and Pools

Barceloneta Beach

There are nine kilometres of beach stretching along Barcelona's coast – Barceloneta is probably the most popular beach.

Nova Icaria

This is a calm, family-friendly beach, just next to Port Olympic. There's some playground equipment and beach-front bars and restaurants (pictured below).

Club Natacio Atletic-Barcelona

A gym complex with lap pools and a play pool set right behind Sant Sebastia beach.

Jardin de la Torre de les Aiges

This public garden and pool is hidden in a courtyard in the Eixample area. It's a sandy park with a shallow pool built at the base of an old water tower.

Wildlife

Zoo

The Parc Zoologic is in Parc de la Ciutadella. It is home to over 5000 animals including dolphins, Komodo dragons, gorillas and Titi monkeys.

Aquarium

The L'Aquarium de Barcelona at Port Vell features a tunnel that you can walk through – with sharks and rays swimming overhead.

Other Stuff

Magic Fountain

Join the crowds and visit the Magic Fountain of Montjuic at night-time to see a fun performance of the fountain shooting water in time to a light and music display.

FC Barcelona Ice Rink

Lace up your skates and take to the ice at the Pista de Gel Olympic-sized ice skating rink at Camp Nou.

Sightseeing Boat Trip

Take a boat from the waterfront area along the coast – you'll get a good view of the city and can spot some major landmarks along the way.

Museums, History and Culture

History and Culture

Montjuic Castle

Montjuic Castle is an old military fortress overlooking the city and the water. There are old cannons, former prison cells and great views from the top of the castle wall. (Castle pictured below.)

Poble Espanyol

A village of 117 full-scale buildings representing different architectural styles from around Spain. The village was built for the 1929 Exposition and was so popular it has remained open ever since.

La Casa dels Entremesos

A cultural centre that is home to many of the giant wearable puppets that join in traditional Catalan festivals. (There are giant puppets inside Santa Maria del Pi and the Palace of Virreina too.)

Catalonia in Minature

Catalunya en Miniatura is a park that is 17 kilometres out of Barcelona. It holds 147 miniature scale models of Catalonian buildings, including all of Gaudi's major works.

Museums

Maritime Museum

At the end of La Rambla, in the old Barcelona Royal Shipyard, the Maritime Museum features large reproduction boats, intricate models and interesting navigational equipment.

Cosmo Caixa

A huge science museum with a geological wall, a planetarium and loads of hands-on activities. It has an indoor rainforest with real birds, frogs and snakes. (Rainforest pictured below.)

Wax Museum

The Museu de Cera is in the old Bank of Barcelona building just off La Rambla. Step into a slightly creepy world and come face to face with historical and fictional characters.

Chocolate Museum

The Museu de la Xocolata is dedicated to the history and production of chocolate. It features statues made of chocolate including a chocolate Sagrada Familia.

THEME PARKS AND CABLE CARS

THEME PARKS

TIBIDABO AMUSEMENT PARK

This historic amusement park is set on top of Tibidabo Mountain, next to the Temple del Sagrat Cor. The park opened way back in 1905. It has some cute old-fashioned rides – the flying red plane ride dates from 1928.

BARCELONA BOSC URBA

This 'Urban Jungle' is an adventure park with zip lining, rope swings, bungee jumping, nets and suspension bridges. There are three circuits for different ages (or different levels of bravery).

ILLA FANTASIA

If it's hot and you need a day off sightseeing, consider a trip out of town to Illa Fantasia Water Park. There are water slides, a wave pool, sandy-beach pools and picnic areas.

CABLE CARS AND FUNICULARS

Barcelona has two cable cars and three funiculars, which can be a fun way to get around. Cable cars are cabins suspended from wires up in the air and funiculars are special trains designed for steep hills.

TRANSBORDADOR AERI DEL PORT

The Port Cable Car travels from San Sebastia beach to Miramar on Montjuic Hill, with great views along the way. Each red and white car holds up to 19 people.

FUNICULAR DE MONTJUIC

This funicular takes you from Parallel metro station to part way up Montjuic Hill. It connects with the Teleferic de Montjuic if you want to ride to the top of the hill.

TELEFERIC DE MONTJUIC

This is a short cable car ride from part way up Montjuic Hill to Montjuic Castle at the top of the hill. Each silver car holds four people.

FUNICULAR DE TIBIDABO

This funicular takes you from Placa del Doctor Andreu up the mountain to Tibidabo Amusement Park.

FUNICULAR DE VALLVIDRERA

This funicular travels from Peu de Funicular to the village of Vallvidrera near the top of Tibidabo Mountain.

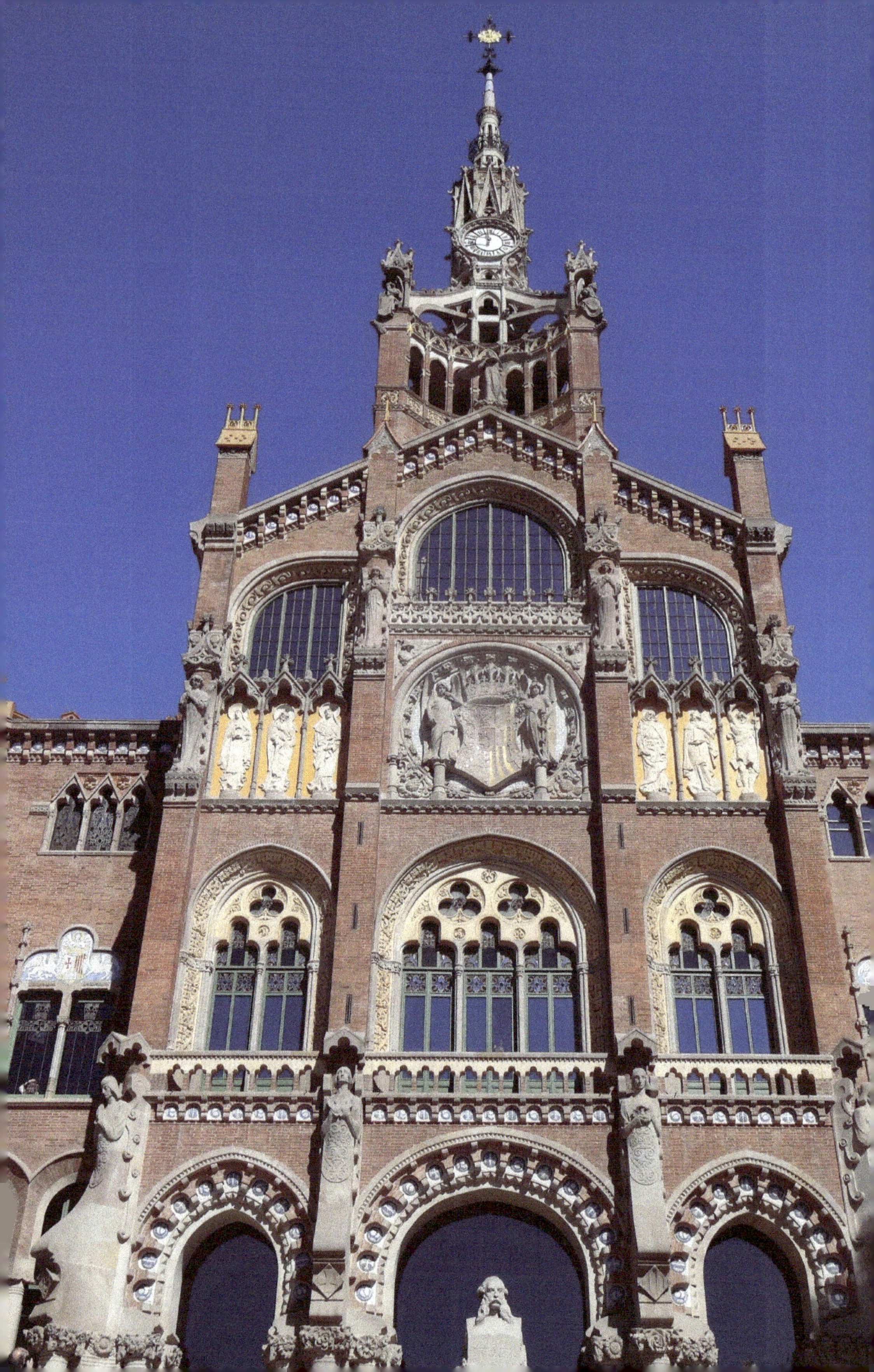

CHAPTER 10

AT THE END

When you are at the end of your trip to Barcelona, tackle this last chapter.

First up, check that you have completed as many of the activities as you can – check the contents page and make sure you have ticked off each completed activity. Is there any left that you can still do?

Next up, finish this chapter. Test your knowledge of Barcelona, pinpoint things on the Barcelona map and think about your favourite (and least favourite) parts of your trip.

Thanks, Barcelona, for a great adventure!

ADIOS Y GRACIAS!

HOSPITAL DE SANT PAU

The building pictured on the facing page is the Hospital de Sant Pau. The building was designed by Lluis Domenech i Montaner and built between 1901 and 1930. (You might remember reading in Chapter 4 that this building is a World Heritage site.)

The building was used as a hospital until 2009 – today it is a museum.

*Photo, left: The facade of the Hospital de Sant Pau.
Right: Mosaic of Saint George at the Hospital de Sant Pau.*

BEST THINGS, WORST THINGS

ACTIVITY 48. @ ANYWHERE

THINK ABOUT EVERYTHING YOU'VE DONE IN BARCELONA

Think about your time in Barcelona: all of the things you did, places you went, food you ate and things you saw.

What were the best things about your time in Barcelona? And what were the worst things? Write down more than one of each.

BEST THINGS

WORST THINGS

MAKE YOUR MAP

ACTIVITY 49. @ ANYWHERE

PLACE THESE BARCELONA LANDMARKS ON THE MAP

See if you can place these fifteen landmarks on this Barcelona map. Then add in any more landmarks that you know.

- Barcelona Cathedral
- Museu Picasso
- Placa de Catalunya
- Casa Vicens
- Columbus Monument
- Parc de la Ciutadella
- Sagrada Familia
- Parc de Joan Miro
- Casa Batllo
- La Boqueria
- Casa Mila
- Magic Fountain
- Placa Reial
- P. de la Musica Catalana
- Arc de Triomf

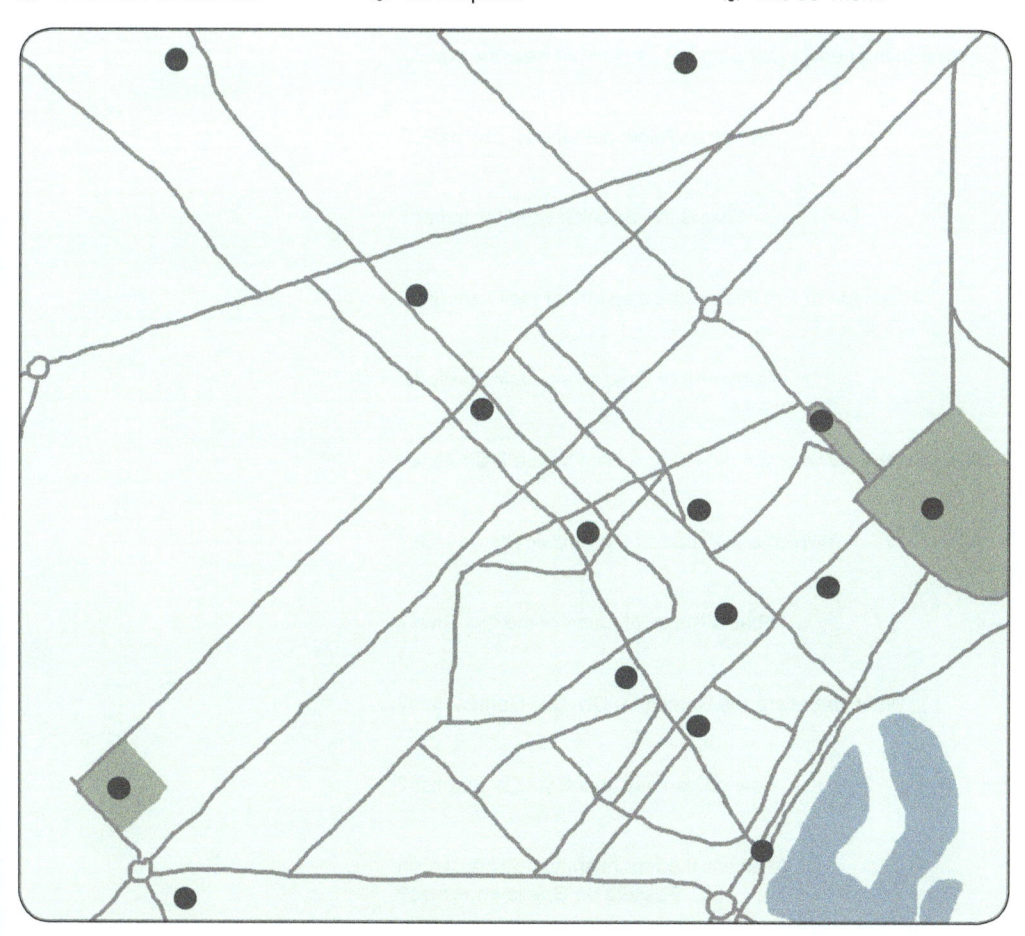

BARCELONA QUIZ

ACTIVITY 50. @ ANYWHERE

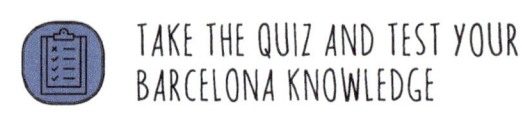

TAKE THE QUIZ AND TEST YOUR BARCELONA KNOWLEDGE

Without looking back through the book, see if you can answer the questions in this quiz. (If you get stuck, try again but this time look back through the book to get help with the answers.)

BONUS QUESTION: HOW MANY YEARS DID GAUDI WORK ON THE SAGRADA FAMILIA FOR?

THE QUIZ

What monument is at the end of La Rambla near the water?

Which architect designed Casa Batllo?

What is the Spanish word for potato?

What type of bird lives in the cloisters of the Cathedral?

Name one of Picasso's painting periods.

What was the name of the old Roman town before Barcelona?

Which artist created the mosaic Pla de L'Os?

What is the local name of the Old Town?

What year were the Barcelona Olympic Games held?

How do you say 'thank you' in Spanish?

What are the four mismatched houses on Passeig de Gracia known as?

CERTIFICATE OF BARCELONA EXPERTISE

CONGRATULATIONS!

THIS IS TO CERTIFY THAT

I, _____ (NAME)

AT THE AGE OF _____

AM OFFICIALLY A BARCELONA EXPERT

AFTER EXPLORING BARCELONA AND COMPLETING THIS BOOK IN

_____ MONTH _____ YEAR.

SIGNED

_____ (SIGN HERE)

EXPERT

YOUR BARCELONA DIARY

Make a note of what you do each day in Barcelona. Write where you went, what you saw and what you ate each day. It will help you to remember your trip.

CHAPTER 11
ANSWERS & CREDITS

ANSWERS TO PUZZLES

ACTIVITY 10

"The only street in the world which I wish...

WOULD NEVER END"

ACTIVITY 11

Portaferrissa
FOUNTAIN

Canaletes
water = aigua
love = enamorats

ACTIVITY 12
>>> NUMBER SEQUENCE

7, 5, 8, 4, 9, 3, ...
Following this pattern: minus 2, add 3, minus 4, add 5, minus 6... the next numbers are: 10, 2, 11, 1, 12, 0

99, 92, 86, 81, 77, ...
Following this pattern: minus 7, minus 6, minus 5, minus 4... the next numbers are: 74, 72, 71

2, 5, 11, 23, 47, ...
Following this pattern: times 2 plus 1, the next numbers are: 95, 191, 383, 767, 1535

ACTIVITY 17

Gaudi's job was:

ARCHITECT

ACTIVITY 20

This picture might help you to find it.

ACTIVITY 26

Picasso's lunch was:

OYSTERS

ACTIVITY 30

Picasso was 76 years old.

ACTIVITY 39
>>> TREES IN A ROW

ACTIVITY 41

Here's just a few:

barnacle, abalone, balance, beacon, carbon, oracle, acorn, alone, bacon, baron, brace, cable, canoe, clean, clear, clone, cobra, enrol, learn, noble, able, area, bare, bean, bear, bone, born, cane, care, cola, cone, core, earn, lace, loan, once, orca, race, robe, role, ace, ale, are, ban, cab, can, cob, con, ear, nab, oar, one, orb, ran, rob

ACTIVITY 45
>>> MINI SUDOKU

Here's one solution:

8	3	4
1	5	9
6	7	2

ACTIVITY 04 - WORD SEARCH

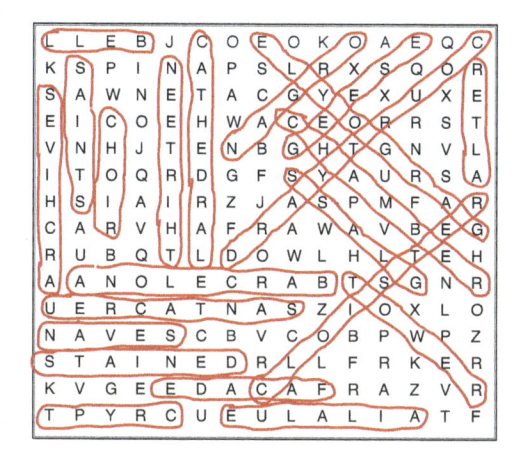

ACTIVITY 43 - MAZE

ACTIVITY 24

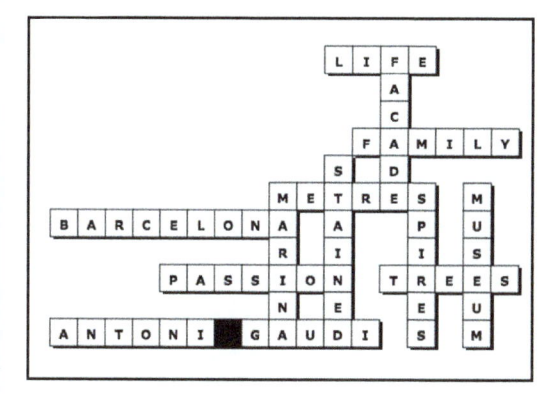

ACTIVITY 33

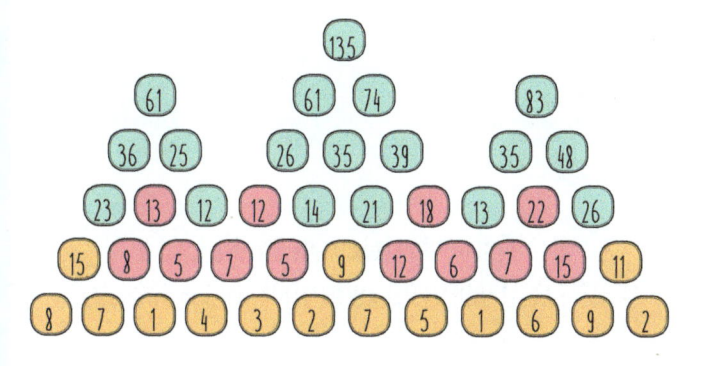

ACTIVITY 46
>>> PET PUZZLE

I have three pets: one dog, one cat and one parakeet.

ACTIVITY 50

Columbus Monument

Antoni Gaudi

Patata

Geese

Blue, Rose, African-Influenced, Cubism, or Crystal

Barcino

Jean Miro

Ciutat Vella (or Barri Gotic at the centre)

1992

Gracias

Block of Discord (or Illa de la Discordia)

Bonus question: 43 years.

THANKS A MILLION TO THESE GUYS

Thanks to Daisy and Graeme for their great ideas, thoughtful edits and enthusiasm. Huge thanks to Debra and Naomi for their excellent advice.

And a massive thank you to the many generous photographers and designers who share their work, credited below.

IMAGE CREDITS

COVER

Cover image of Casa Batllo: 495756
Pencil drawing: created by Alex Muravev from Noun Project

CH 1 - HELLO BARCELONA

Title page
Sculpture at Park Guell: pblotlefevre
View from Palau Nacional: Wjh31
The rest
Market sweets: Joaquin Aranoa

Activity icons
Speech bubble icon: created by logan from Noun Project

CH 2 - THE OLD TOWN

Title page:
Pont del Bisbe: 495756
Hercules statue: Yearofthedragon
The Ancient Roman City of Barcino
Temple of August drawing: Carole Raddato
Barcino stone: jaycross
Barri Gotic Walking Tour
Placa Nova: Maria Rosa Ferre
Font de Santa Ana: Canaan
Casa de L'Ardiaca: AngelaLlop
Cathedral de Barcelona: Bracons
Temple D'August: Enfo
Placa Sant Jaume: Alberto
Pont del Bisbe: Tony Hisgett
Monument to Heroes: Enfo
Placa de Sant Felip Neri: Enfo
Cathedral Creature Hunter
Gargoyles left to right top row: Pere Lopez, Bernard Gagnan
Gargoyles left to right bottom row: Pere Lopez, Pere Lopez, Bernard Gagnan
Geese: Jerzy Gorecki
Ciutadella Landmarks
Font de la Cascada: Artanderson
Medallons del Ilangardaix: Enfo
Neptune: Enfo
Castell de Tres Dragons: Selbymay
Mammoth Sculpture: Selbymay
Deconsol: Enfo

Arc de Triomf Photo Locator
Arc photos clockwise from top left: Katerina198, Diosringas, no credit, Eugeniomondejar.
Waterfront Alpha-challenge
Barceloneta beach: AmaO

Activity icons
Eye icon: created by Alina Oleynik from Noun Project
Map icon: created by Hopkins from Noun Project
Sneakers icon: created by Madeleine Bennett from Noun Project
Binoculars icon: created by Joe Pictos from Noun Project
Pencil icon: created by Jesper Vestergaard from Noun Project
Fountain icon: created by Made by Made from Noun Project
Camera icon: created by Alpha Design from Noun Project
Waves icon: created by Oksana Latysheva from Noun Project

CH 3 - LA RAMBLA

Title page
La Rambla: Xibber
Street performer: Laslovarga
Find These La Rambla Landmarks
Placa de Catalunya: Freepenguin
Font de la Canaletes: Enfo
Font de la Portaferrissa: Canaan
Palau de la Virreina: Kippelboy
La Boqueria: Oleksandr Samoylyk
Pla de L'Os Mosaic: Eric
Gran Teatre del Liceu: Enfo
Placa Reial: Freepenguin

Activity icons
Eye icon: created by Alina Oleynik from Noun Project
Shoe icon: created by H Alberto Gongora from Noun Project
Magnifying glass icon: created by Juan Carlos Altamirano from Noun Project
Font plaque icons, left and right: created by Arthur Shlain from Noun Project
Apple icon: created by Creative Stall from Noun Project
Question icon: created by Pham Thi Dieu Linh from Noun Project
Watermelon icon: created by Iconic from Noun Project

CH 4 - GAUDI & MODERNISM

Title page
Casa Batllo: 495756
Ceramics: Enfo
Palau Guell's Gates
Palau Guell gate: Seth Lemmons
Architecture Walking Tour
Tile detail from Casa Amatller: Amadalvarez
Casa Lleo Morera: Amadalvarez
Casa Mullarus: Xavier Badia Castella
Casa Amatller: Strecosa
Casa Batllo: Rhiannon
Casa Mila: Violetta
El Palauet: Perepripz
Casa Fuster: Jaume Meneses
Casa Vicens: Jaume Meneses
Craftspeople who worked with Gaudi
Ceramic: Amadalvarez
Stained glass: Amadalvarez
Mosaic: LoggaWiggler
Palau de la Musica Catalana
Palau interior: Wang
Design a concert ticket
Ticket window: Enfo
Guell Treasure Hunt
Round images clockwise from top: Travelkr; Ardfern; LoggaWiggler; Delia Lendeczki; Maria Michelle; LoggaWiggler
Make Your Own Mosaic
Mosaic: Gozitano

Activity icons
Binoculars icon: created by Joe Pictos from Noun Project
Palette icon: created by Symbolon from Noun Project
Map icon: created by Hopkins from Noun Project
Pencil icon: created by Hopkins from Noun Project
Shoes icon: created by Madeleine Bennett from Noun Project
Calculator icon: created by AFY Studio from Noun Project
Ticket icon: created by Awesome from Noun Project
Treasure chest icon: created by Focus Lab from Noun Project
Crayon icon: created by Becris from Noun Project
Eye icon: created by Alina Oleynik from Noun Project

WE'D REALLY APPRECIATE AN ONLINE REVIEW: LITTLETRAVELGUIDES.COM.AU OR YOUR ONLINE BOOKSHOP

CH 5 - SAGRADA FAMILIA

Title page
View of Passion Facade: Marianitapansi90
Roped worker: DagafeSQV
Orientation walk
Nativity facade: Nikolai_Karaneschev
Interior view of columns: Antoni63
Passion Facade sculpture face: Philip Serracino Inglott
Apse windows: Sagrada Familia Official
Scavenger Hunt
Star of Bethlehem: Böhringer Friedrich
Donkey: Turol Jones
Magi: Turol Jones
Maria: Sagrada Familia Official
Basket: Turol Jones
Magic Square: Ad Meskens
Jesus on door: Turol Jones
Alpha and Omega symbol: Etantjal
Soldier with sword: Turol Jones
Papal Plaque: Jordiferrer
Papal coat of arms: Serge Melki
Floor etching: Little Savage
Door of Charity leaves: Canaan
Sheaf door detail: Dvdgmz
Snails: Jordiferrer
Emblem of St Luke: José Luiz Bernardes Ribeiro
Turtle under pillar: Stanislav Kozlovskiy
Museum illustration by Josep Subirachs: Balou46
Candelabra: José Luiz Bernardes Ribeiro
Catenary arch model: Rüdiger Marmulla
Model of Passion Facade: José Luiz Bernardes Ribeiro
The Stained Glass Windows
Windows, left: Jean-Christophe Benoist
Windows, right: Tony Hisgett
Under construction: Sguastevi
Building the Sagrada Familia
Gaudi sculpture: Yair Haklai

Activity icons
Sagrada Familia icon: created by David Padrosa from Noun Project
Eye icon: created by Alina Oleynik from Noun Project
Pencil icon: created by Oliviu Stoian from Noun Project
Crossword icon: created by Luka Purgar from Noun Project

FOUND A MISTAKE?
A PAINTING NOT THERE?
A STATUE MOVED?
PLEASE LET US KNOW.
HI.LITTLETRAVELGUIDES
@GMAIL.COM

CH 6 - MUSEU PICASSO

Title page
Museum sign: Moheenreeyad
Pigeon Mathematics
Museum building, Palau Aguilar: Kippelboy

Activity icons
3D building icon: created by Artem Kovyazin from Noun Project
Painting icon: created by Nancy from Noun Project
Palette icon: created by Symbolon from Noun Project
Magnifying glass icon: created by Juan Carlos Altamirano from Noun Project
Crayon icon: created by Becris from Noun Project
Pigeon icon: created by Nicholas Menghini from Noun Project
Paper and pencil icon: created by Stock Image Folio from Noun Project

CH 7 - MONTJUIC HILL

Title page
Jardi Botanic: Daderot
Barcelona View Finder
Palau Nacional: Briggs321
Magic Fountain Number Puzzle
Magic Fountain: Till F Teenck
Parkland Nature Bingo
Jardi Botanic: Daderot
Cable Car view: Gustavo de la Sota
More About Montjuic
Miro mural: Kippelboy
Fundacio Jean Miro: Felix Konig
Montjuic Castle: Jorge Franganillo

Activity icons
Binoculars icon: created by Joe Pictos from Noun Project
Calculator icon: created by AFY Studio from Noun Project
Leaf icon: created by Arthur Schlain from Noun Project
Butterfly icon: created by Focus Lab from Noun Project
Crayons icon: created by Becris from Noun Project

CH 8 - ACROSS BARCELONA

Title page
Sant Raphael: Enfo
Santa Maria del Mar: Benutzer Bautsch
Spot That Shape
Santa Maria del Pi: Andriy Sadivskyy
Giant puppets: Pere Lopez
Energy Burn Challenge
Basilica de la Merce statue: Jordiferrer
Pubic Art Treasure Hunt
Picasso Friezes: Ktanaka
Barcelona Face: Piper60
The Fish: Isiwal
Woman and Bird: Gerardo Nunez
Raval Cat: Canaan
Wounded Falling Star: Martin Abegglen
Gambrinus: Mutari
Thinking Bull: Beroesz
Stargazers: Fabio Alessandro Locati
Homage to Swimming: Enfo
Barcino: Enfo
Find Camp Nou Maze
Cathedral: Bracons
Camp Nou: Clicjeroen
Draw a Barcelona Building
Temple Expiatori del Sagrat Cor: Slisicin
Hotel Olympics
Sant Pau del Camp: TenofallTrades

Activity icons
Shapes icon: created by Icon 54 from Noun Project
Battery icon: created by Lipi from Noun Project
Binoculars icon: created by Joe Pictos from Noun Project
Thinking icon: created by Eucalyp from Noun Project
Cutlery icon: created by Chiara Galli from Noun Project
Maze icon: created by Juan Pablo Bravo from Noun Project
Box icon: created by Ralf Schmitzer from Noun Project
Tick box icon: created by Kimmi Studio from Noun Project
Pencil icon: created by Hopkins from Noun Project
Olympic rings icon: created by Plastic Donut from Noun Project

CH 9 - BARCELONA FOR KIDS

Title page
Tibidabo Ferris Wheel: Lobito
Indian Peafowl: Mutari
Camp Nou: Puppet
The rest
Jardins de Joan Brossa: Alexander Kachkaev
Park del Laberint D'Horta: Josemanuel
Nova Icaria Beach: Freepenguin
Montjuic Castle: Puigalder
Cosmo Caixa Rainforest: Alberto G Rovi
Port Cable Car: Anemone123

CH 10 - AT THE END

Title page
Hospital de Sant Pau: Jordiferrer
Saint George mosaic: Oliver Bonjoch

Activity icons
Thumbs up and down: created by Cards Against Humanity from Noun Project
Map pointer: created by Andrey Vasiliev from Noun Project
Checklist: created by Made from Noun Project

CH 11 - ANSWERS & CREDITS

Mosaic: Gozitano
Question icon: created by Pham Thi Dieu Linh from Noun Project
Heart smiley icon: created by Vectors Market from Noun Project